Tomorrow We Live

Oswald Mosley

Tomorrow We Live

Oswald Mosley

First Published 1938
This Edition: 2019

Copyright © 2019 Sanctuary Press Ltd

ISBN-13: 978-1-913176-26-6

Sanctuary Press Ltd
71-75 Shelton Street
Covent Garden
London
WC2H 9JQ

www.sanctuarypress.com
Email: info@sanctuarypress.com

Contents

Introduction

A BOOK of thirty-four thousand words can serve the reader only as an introduction to the spirit and policy of British Union.

The subject is too great to be confined in all detail within such limits of space. But the reader who inquires further will discover in the publications of the British Union an amplitude of detail on every subject of the day. Books and pamphlets by my colleagues, whose range of abilities now cover every sphere of national life, will meet any inquiry, and further detail on some topics can be found in my own books, "*The Greater Britain*" and "*100 Questions Answered.*"

In these pages the reader will discover, with the exception of the chapter on Foreign Affairs, a policy suited to the character of this country and no other. British Union in whole character is a British principle suited to Britain alone. It is true that our National Socialist and Fascist creed is universal, in different form and method, to all great countries of the modern world. That was true also in their own period of every great creed, political or religious, that our country has ever known. The only difference in this respect between British Union and the old parties is that our creed belongs to the twentieth century, and their creeds to the past that conceived them. But a greater difference arises from the fact that National Socialism and Fascism is in essence a national doctrine which finds in each great nation a character, policy, form and method suited to each particular country. For this reason a far greater divergence will be found in the expression and method of the modern Movement in different countries than prevailed in the case of the international creeds of the past such as Liberalism and Socialism, or Conservatism, which, under various names, can be found in every country in the world.

So the reader will find in these pages a policy born only of British inspiration, and a character and method suited to Britain alone. He will be able to judge for himself our claim for British Union that in constructive conception our policy already far transcends any previous emanation of the modern Movement. We do not borrow ideas from foreign countries and we have no "models" abroad for a plain and simple reason. We are proud enough of our own people to believe that once Britain is awake our people will not follow, but will lead mankind. In this deep faith we hold that no lesser destiny is worthy of the British people than that the whole world shall find in Britain an example. The aim of British Union is no less than this.

Oswald Mosley

System of Government –
What is Wrong ?

Financial Democracy

THE will of the people shall prevail. The policy for which the people have voted shall be carried out. This is the essence of good government in an enlightened age. This is the principle which is denied by the system misnamed democracy, which in degeneration is more appropriately called financial democracy. The reason is that government is paralysed by the maintenance of a parliamentary system a century out of date. When the Government elected by the people is incapable of rapid and effective action private and vested interests assume the real power of Government, not by vote or permission of the people, but by power of money dubiously acquired.

In recent years the trifling measures which have struggled through parliamentary obstruction have been insignificant in their effect on the lives of the people by comparison with the immense exercise of money power. Decisions and movements of international finance on Wall Street, and its sub-branch in the City of London, may send prices soaring to create a speculator's paradise at the expense of the real wages of the people, or may send prices crashing to throw millions into unemployment as the aftermath of some gigantic gamble. In terms of the things that really matter to the people, such as real wages, employment, the hours of labour, food prices, and the simple ability to pay the rent, finance, under the present system, can affect the lives of the mass of the people more closely and more terribly in the decision of one afternoon than can Parliament, with puny labour and the mock heroics of sham battles, in the course of a decade. For the instrument of the money power was designed to fit present conditions and to exploit the decadence of an obsolete system. Parliament, on the other hand, was created long before modern conditions existed to meet an altogether different set of facts.

New Conditions

Parliamentary Government, practically in modern form, was designed primarily to prevent the abuse of elementary liberties in a relatively simple rural community with a primitive national economy. The facts of that age have no relation to the periods of steam and power, which were followed swiftly by vast accumulations of finance capital that possess the unlimited international mobility of a world force. Is it really likely that the parliamentary instrument of a century or more ago should be equally suitable to meet the facts of an age which science has revolutionised? Yet on the assumption that the system of government alone required no change, during the century of most startling change that mankind has known, rests the policy and the philosophy of every one of the old parties of the State, Conservative, Liberal and Labour alike!

This patent fallacy which all the old parties teach the people admirably suits the financial exploiter. A parliamentary system devised to check personal outrages by medieval courts or nobles is represented still as the effective guardian of liberty in this age of international finance. It would be as true to say that the bow and arrow with which primitive man defended his farm from the marauding wolf is equally effective to defend him against the tanks of a modern invading army. But the people are persuaded that the instruments by which they preserved some semblance of liberty in the past are still effective to preserve their liberties in modern conditions, in order that these liberties may be taken from them without their loss even being realised.

Parliament and Liberty

It suits our financial masters well that all parties should combine to tell the people that Parliament is the sole effective guardian of liberty, and, naturally, the national Press, which the money power so largely controls, is in unison to echo the same refrain. It is also not surprising to find that anyone who dares to suggest that the liberty of the people alone can be preserved, and their will alone can be carried out, by the entrusting of the Government, which they have elected, with power in the name of the people to act, should be unanimously denounced by the old parties and by the financial Press as a tyrant who desires to overthrow British liberty. As long as the people can be gulled into the belief that they are free today so long can their slavery be perpetuated. Therefore, every instrument of the financial tyranny from party machines to national Press is mobilised behind a barrage of money power to resist the simple principle that power belongs to the people alone, and that their power can only be expressed by giving their freely chosen Government the power to act.

That such power in Government does not exist today can scarcely be denied. It is admitted that only two big Bills can be passed through Parliament in the course of a whole year, which means that any effective programme submitted as a pledge of immediate action to the electorate would take more than the lifetime of a generation to carry out.

Under such conditions every election programme becomes a fraudulent prospectus, which, contrary to the experience of business life, carries the most fraudulent not to gaol, but to Downing Street. Every main Bill has four stages of debate on the floor of the House of Commons alone, and in two stages can be debated line by line by a committee of over six hundred people. In such circumstances the ability of the Opposition to obstruct is unlimited, and no measure can in effect reach the Statute Book in face of really determined opposition. The result is that bargain, compromise, and delay completely stultify the programme for which the majority of the people have voted. Yet this is the procedure which we are told "honest" men are prepared to operate, within a system which renders impossible the execution of the promises which they have given to the people, and by means of which they have secured office and power.

The First Duty

On the contrary, we ask whether any honest man or Movement in politics would not make his first proposal and his first duty to create an instrument of Government by which he could carry out the promises he had made and the policy for which the people have voted. Yet all the old parties combine to resist this principle of elementary honesty, and to denounce as the denial of liberty any suggestion to give to the people the first principle of liberty in the actual execution of the policy they desire. As a result the vote becomes ever more meaningless, and fewer people take the trouble to exercise it as they learn by bitter experience that, no matter the party for which they vote, they never by any chance secure the policy for which they have voted. Farcical becomes the parliamentary scene as the people realise that in a dynamic age this system can never deliver the goods, and like all systems in decline the parliamentary mind seems anxious only to produce its own caricature.

In the Light of history it will ever be regarded as a curious and temporary aberration of the human mind that great nations should elect a Government to do a job and should then elect an Opposition to stop them doing it. Fortunately, even in the wildest excesses of this transient mania, this delusion never spread to the business world, and no business man outside an asylum has yet been observed to engage a staff of six to carry on the work of his firm, and then to engage an additional staff of four to stop them doing their job. Curious to posterity will appear the principle of creating at the same time a Government to do the nation's work and an Opposition to frustrate it. But stranger still will seem the final reduction to absurdity of the parliamentary system whereby a Prime Minister is paid £10,000 a year to do the nation's job, and the Leader of the Opposition is paid, and accepts, £2,000 a year of the nation's money to stop him doing it. Yet this extraordinary harlequinade, in which nothing serious, in terms of the modern mind, is ever done, and little serious is even discussed, is today represented as the only means of preserving the liberties of the people.

The instruments by which this great racket has been achieved are plain to see. The first is the maintenance of an obsolete parliamentary system still invested from a past of difficult conditions with the myth of liberty, by means of which Government is paralysed in order that the real power of Government may be exercised elsewhere, not by the chosen of the people but by the chosen of finance. The second instrument is the monopoly of propaganda by the money power in the shape of a Press also invested with the myth of liberty from a past of different conditions. The Free Press built by genuine journalists who were vendors of honest "news" long ago gave place in most of the national Press to the financial combine which acquires control of great blocks of newspaper shares. So the money power again in the name of a Free Press can serve to the people not only the opinions but also the "news" which serves the interests of the money power. Not only are our "free" British denied any meaning to the vote in the shape of ever getting what they want, but they are also denied even the small privilege of learning the truth. For power and propaganda alike are in the hands of a force whose interests conflict with the interests of the people and is careful that they should not even learn the truth. Thus the myth of freedom in Parliament and Press combine to promote the slavery of the people.

Finance Power

Most of the Press is owned outright by the money power, or is controlled by the advertisements which money power controls, and Parliament is paralysed by talk that power may reside elsewhere. But the argument may be taken further, for the economic system which is maintained by finance power for the benefit of its own interests, and to the detriment of every interest of the people, also ensures that any Government may at any time be broken by the money power. The international economic system is supported by every party of the State, Conservative, Liberal and Labour alike. It will be shown in detail in chapter three of this book that this system enables any Government to be broken at any time by the financial power, as the weak Socialist Government was broken in Britain in 1931, and the weak Socialist Government of Blum was broken in France in 1937.

It was not enough for finance to dope the system of Government with the talkative parliamentary system of a century ago. Finance in the economic system also retains the power at any time to knock a Government on the head. By way of further precaution the finance of the money power controls the party machines, which in their turn control Parliament and Government.

So this is finality in the land of "liberty and free speech":

1. Government is paralysed by the system of talk that power may reside elsewhere;

2. Government can at any time be destroyed by the power of money alone;

3. the Press which controls opinion is itself largely controlled by the money power;

4. the party machines which control even the right of the individual to make a speech to an appreciable audience in public are also controlled by the money power.

So what is left to you "free Britons" to voice your opinion and make your will effective? You can go into a public-house and grumble in the assurance that no one will take the slightest notice of what you say. But even then you must be sure to be out in the streets by closing time, because the Old Woman of Westminster prefers, even in your private life, to treat you as a child rather than as a man.

There stands the Briton in the street, gulled into the acceptance of slavery by words about liberty, and boasting of freedom, while in truth denied the freedom to call his own even the soul of which alone his masters have not robbed him, for the simple reason that it has no cash value.

Is that really the Briton - tricked, fooled, hagridden, exploited, enslaved? Or does a generation arise again, breaking from the hands of manhood resurgent the fetters of decadence and seeing with the ardent eyes of an awakened giant the land that they shall make their own.

British Union System Of Government

British Union Movement

THE will of the people shall prevail. The policy for which the people have voted shall be carried out. This is the essence of British Union Government. In the previous chapter the present complete frustration of the people's will has been examined and the formidable instruments of that frustration have been surveyed. In cold fact the money power commands Government, Parliament, Party Machinery and Press. Not only does it possess the power to render Government impotent and, if necessary, to break Government; money power also possesses the means of preventing any new opinion or even any true news from reaching the people at all. Faced with this formidable power and almost limitless corruption of a decadent system, those who founded the British Union were moved by the deep belief that from the people themselves alone could be created the instrument by which freedom could be won for the people, and by which our country could be redeemed to greatness. Such an instrument clearly, in its whole character and structure, must differ from the old parties of the State.

It would be idle with infinite labour to create a new movement to combat current corruption of such a loose and flaccid character that, like the revolutionary movements of the immediate past, it would fall an easy victim to the very corruption that it was designed to destroy. If this basic principle is understood, much in the history and character of our Movement that has been misunderstood will be easily comprehended. We had to create an "instrument of steel" because we know from our experience of democracy that any character less hard and tested would easily succumb to the system that it was designed to combat. Consequently our Movement has rested from the outset upon the principles of struggle, sacrifice, and voluntary discipline. In the fire of that struggle and by the force of the sacrifice for which I have never called in vain, the "instrument of steel" has been forged that shall cut through corruption to a larger freedom than this land has ever known.

It has been forged from the heart and soul of the people alone in the sacrifice of thousands of unknown but utterly devoted men and women who have been ready to give all that Britain might live.

This Movement has been created by simple people in face of money power, party power, and press power without any aid from the great names of the present system, and in face of every weapon of boycott and misrepresentation that the money power could mobilise. Thus ever have been born the great determinist forces of history in face of all material things by the force of the spirit alone.

So has been accomplished the first stage in the mission of regeneration which is the creation from the people themselves and from the people alone of a Movement capable of leading the mass of the people to freedom. Those who sacrifice all for an undying cause are inevitably a minority even in the movement they create. Soon thousands came and now come who are gladly welcomed to give support or any kind of service, but many of whom for innumerable reasons, domestic and business, are inhibited from the supreme sacrifice that builds this Movement. Still later a whole nation will give support with enthusiasm to a cause that has been built through the sacrifice by pioneers of most that makes life dear to men.

But they who lead the people to a higher civilisation are ever those who are capable of supreme self dedication. The authority of leadership carries with it the responsibility of such a life. Thus our new leaders of the people in every area of the land have been discovered, tried, and tested in the actual ordeal of struggle. Their sacrifice during a struggle harder and fiercer in its whole nature than any movement has known before in this country is the guarantee to the people that they will not again be betrayed. Men and women do not sacrifice all in order to betray the thing to which they have given their lives. A Fascist who, in power after such a struggle, betrayed his cause, would betray his own life blood. Thus the struggle of a National Socialist Movement is a necessary preliminary to the exercise of power, because the bitter character of that struggle gives to the people an absolute guarantee that those who have passed through that test unbroken will not betray their people or their country. Thus alone is forged the "instrument of steel" to save and then to serve the people.

The Leadership Principle

The rebirth of a nation comes from the people in a clear and ordered sequence. The People, their Movement, their Government, their Power. To create their Government and to overthrow the Government of the money power which oppresses them the people have first to create their Movement. This act enables them for the first time to give meaning to the vote by electing their Government to power. The final stage is to arm this Government with power in their name to act.

To represent this process as the constitution of a dictatorship against the will of the people is a travesty of the facts as dishonest as it is childish. The only dictatorship that we propose for this country is the dictatorship of the people themselves, which shall replace the present dictatorship of the vested interests. Our Movement offers to the people not dictatorship but leadership through an instrument by which their will can be carried out. British Union and leadership seek not to be dictator to the people but servant of the people.

The only stipulation that we make is the simple condition that if the people want us to do the job they shall give us the power to do it. Is that unreasonable? Is it not a waste of the people's time and money to create a Government which has not the power to act? Is it not simple dishonesty for any man or movement to accept office without the power to act and without the ability to perform what he has undertaken to do?

Our principle is the leadership principle which has nothing whatever to do with dictatorship. It is true that this principle is the opposite to the collective irresponsibility of the "democratic" committee system but that does not make it dictatorship. British Union believes in the following simple principles: (1) give a man a job to do; (2) give him the power to do it; (3) hold him responsible for doing it; (4) sack him if he does not do it. Our principles, therefore, are neither dictatorship nor the fugitive irresponsibility of a committee. We have seen the committee system in action within financial democracy and have observed its consequence. If several men are in name responsible no one is, in fact, responsible, and no one can be held to account for failure.

Everyone shelters behind his colleagues and disclaims personal responsibility; all wanted to do the right thing, but none could persuade their colleagues to do it. Not only does the committee system of financial democracy dissipate action in endless talk; it breeds cowardice and evasion in leadership in place of courage and responsibility. Therefore, in the building of our Movement and in the building of a Government we believe in the leadership principle, which means personal and individual responsibility.

Whether a man occupies a position of minor responsibility or a position of the gravest responsibility in the State that task is his responsibility and that of no other, and for the execution of that task he shall be held responsible to the people. Authority can never be divided because divided authority means divided responsibility, and that leads to the futility and cowardice of the committee system. Failure to comprehend this principle is failure alike to understand the principles of National Socialism or the essence of any creed of dynamic action and achievement since the world began. But to represent as dictatorship authority freely conferred by the people in return for the manly acceptance of personal responsibility is a misunderstanding, or rather misrepresentation, equally gross.

In the building of our Movement and the creation of our Government the principle is leadership, and not dictatorship, for plain and obvious reasons. No one can be compelled to join our Movement and any member can walk out of it any day he likes if he does not accept its principles or leadership. He is perfectly free to try to do better himself in the creation and conduct of another movement. In this country, as in others, many tried their hand until the confusion of little societies with imitative policies and inflated egotisms faded away in the advance of British Union to be a National Movement, by the simple test of alone possessing the capacity to attract a national following. It is idle, therefore, to argue that prior to the winning of power our Movement rests on the dictatorship principle for none need belong to it who do not wish. After the winning of power equally it rests not on dictatorship but on the leadership principle, for power is conferred by the free vote of the people and can be removed by the free vote of the people.

The Structure of Government

British Union seeks power by the vote of the people alone at a general election. But we tell the people quite frankly in advance that we will not accept responsibility without power, because we believe it to be dishonest to take office without the ability to carry out the policy for which the people have voted. The first measure of British Union Government will, therefore, be a General Powers Bill conferring on Government the means to act by order, subject to the right of Parliament elected by the vote of the people at any time to dismiss the Government by vote of censure if it abuses power. Subject to this right of dismissal by Parliament the Government will be free to act without delay or obstruction from the interminable rigmarole of present parliamentary procedure. Parliament will be called together at regular intervals to review the work of the Government and to criticise and suggest. M.P.s will be armed with facts for criticism and suggestion which they do not at present possess, because they will not spend most of their time in the corrupting atmosphere of Westminster but in the stimulating atmosphere of their own constituencies among the people whom they represent. In particular British Union will give most of the M.P.s an executive task in place of a purely talkative role in a complete reform of the local authority system. Local authority areas will be enlarged and all purely local matters will be delegated to their jurisdiction. Again, the leadership principle will be employed and the executive leader of the local authority will be an M.P. of the majority party in Parliament elected from the area over whose local authority he presides. He will be advised and assisted by a local Council elected on the principle of occupational franchise, the method of which both local and national will be described later in this chapter. Each member of the Council will be an executive officer in charge of a Local Government department and responsible to the local leader, who will be responsible to the Government of the nation. Thus committee irresponsibility in local, as in national affairs, will yield place to the leadership principle of personal responsibility and effective action.

Local leaders both in the first Parliament of British Union and in the permanent system will be selected from the Movement for which the majority of the people have voted. To many this may seem a revolutionary principle but, in fact, is it not plain common sense? Local leaders will be selected as ministers are today from the party for which the majority of the country have voted and will be given power to act. Can Government ever be effective or action ever be taken if differing policies are pursued by National Government and local authority? What would happen to a business whose head office pursued one policy and whose branch offices pursued another? Can any real democrat object to the principle that the programme for which the majority of the people have voted shall be carried out both nationally and locally? We hear so much these days of the rights of the minority that many are inclined to forget the rights of the majority. Is it democracy or any form of free government for the majority of the people to vote for a programme which is completely frustrated not only by obstruction at Westminster but by minority obstruction also in hundreds of different and conflicting local Councils? In practice financial democracy means that in the name of minority rights the right of the majority is invariably denied. British Union policy rests on the simple principle that nationally and locally the will of the majority of the people shall prevail. The incidental advantage of the execution of this principle is that the majority of M.P.s are saved from the demoralising chatter of the House of Commons lobbies and given an executive task with personal responsibility that will evoke from the people's representatives the capacities requisite to a man of action. No process is more necessary to the creation of effective government than to transmute the people's representatives from mere talkers into men of action.

Many a good revolutionary has arrived at Westminster roaring like a lion, only a few months later to be cooing as the tame dove of his opponents. The bar, the smoking room, the lobby, the dinner tables of his constituents' enemies, and the "atmosphere of the best club in the country," very quickly rob a people's champion of his vitality and fighting power. Revolutionary movements lose their revolutionary ardour as a result long before they ever reach power, and the warrior of the platform becomes the lapdog of the lobbies. In the light of this experience British Union M.P.s from the outset will go to Westminster under solemn pledge not to mix socially, or even to speak, to their opponents. They will go to Parliament to fight for the people who sent them there, and not to fraternise with men who have betrayed the people.

Thus only with sustained fighting spirit and revolutionary ardour can the nation's cause be served. In Westminster, as outside, British Union must be the "instrument of steel" in the service of the people. Until we win power we shall fight every inch of the way, and directly upon the winning of power we shall establish an instrument of Government capable of executing the people's will. This instrument, nationally and locally, will be created by the vote of the majority of the people and this instrument, nationally and locally, will execute their will. Power conferred by the people in their name will be exercised, and that power shall be removed by the vote of the people alone, to whom alone, under the Crown, we will account and be responsible.

Occupational Franchise

We have observed that in the first Parliament of British Union complete power of action by Government is combined with the right of Parliament elected by the people to dismiss the Government if it abuses power. Government's power of action nationally and locally is complete, but so also the control of the people over Government is complete.

We come now to the consideration of the permanent system which is created with the second Parliament of British Union. The first Parliament, by necessity, is elected on the existing franchise which is geographical. That franchise is a relic of the past, in which the interests of men and women were more centred in their locality of residence than in their occupation within the national economy. Such conditions have long passed away as the main categories of occupation assumed a national in place of a purely local character. Today the fact that a man is an engineer or doctor, a farmer or cotton operative, is a greater factor in his existence than the particular locality in which he happens to reside. In modern and scientific organisation occupation definitely supersedes in importance the chance of residence. In geographical constituencies thousands of diverse human beings and interests are fortuitously brought together by the franchise without much knowledge of each other and with few interests in common. Again this system of voting in its obsolescence produces the abuses of decay.

Early electorates of a less complex age could discriminate in giving a vote on simple national issues for one or other local leader whose character and views were well known to them. An election with the vast modern electorate is a very different matter as the great network of national questions is far too complex for any but whole time specialists thoroughly to understand, and the personalities and real views of the candidates can only be known at all to a fraction of the voters. The confusion of a present election under the old system lends itself to the charlatan candidate employing the catchword of the moment without any relation either to the reality of national issues or to the policies which he subsequently supports in Parliament. In such circumstances the slick talker generally defeats the serious worker, and the divorce between promise and subsequent performance leads increasingly to the Wholesale disillusion of the electorate.

It is, therefore, necessary to restore not only reality but understanding to the vote. The idea that all men on all subjects are equally competent to give a verdict becomes, in modern conditions, an ever more manifest absurdity. Therefore, we propose an occupational franchise that men and women may vote on problems they well understand for personnel with whom they have a long familiarity.

Men and women will vote not as residents in a particular locality but as persons engaged in a particular occupation. Doctors will vote as doctors, engineers as engineers, miners as miners, farmers as farmers, farm workers as farm workers, married women as housewives and mothers with a franchise of their own.

Women's Part

It is noteworthy today that the mothers of the nation possess few representatives in Parliament with any special competence to represent them. Women's questions are usually handled by ageing spinsters, for the simple reason that most women with any practical experience of maternity find the conflict between home and public life so intolerable that they retire again to a sphere where their true interests lie. The problem can only be resolved by occupational franchise, which gives them special representation in a Parliament that will not remove them altogether from the interests they represent.

The care of the mother and the child is one of the main neglects of the present system and will be among the main concerns of British Union. It is only right, therefore, that this great interest should secure proper representation with the other great interests of the nation. This does not mean that we seek to relegate women purely to the home, which is a charge denied in practice by the act that we present today a larger proportion of women candidates to the electorate than any other party. In our permanent system women in industry or the professions will have their vote and their representatives within their occupation. An economic system which provides work for all has no need to drive women from industry. But a political system which guards the health and strength of the race will certainly prevent the grave scandal of women being driven from the home against their will because the miserable wages of the men cannot keep the home together. Women, whether in home or industry, will hold a high and honoured place in accord with British tradition and will receive full measure of representation and weight in the counsels of the State.

End of the Party Game

Occupational franchise, therefore, will secure a technical Parliament suited to the problems of a technical age. A vote given with full information and, consequently, with a sense of responsibility will secure a serious and dignified assembly. Such a Parliament will consider national questions freely on their merits and not beneath the lash of the party whip in the ignoble scramble for place which has become the hallmark of present politics. It is clear that such a system brings to an end the party game and apart from other advantages it is deliberately designed to that end. British Union means to bring to an end the party game. There is no time in the modern world, with menacing problems of a dynamic age for mere opposition for the sake of opposing, in the hope of getting the other man's job by the simple process of blacking his face by any means, fair or foul.

Under our system a man or woman will be elected because he, or she, is a good engineer or a good doctor, not a party doctor or party engineer. The M.P. will emerge to prominence and office not by dexterity in mere debate, or by bibulous capacity to sit up all night to obstruct the business of the nation, but by serious criticism and constructive suggestion which will make real contribution to the deliberations of the nation. In a new age the party type will pass, together with the corruption of the party machine.

People's Control Over Government

Few will deny that the constructive seriousness of such a Parliament will be an improvement on the frivolity and chicanery of an obsolete system. But the question is often raised how, in the absence of organised opposition, the people can change the Government if they wish. The answer is that in the permanent system of British Union the life of the Government will depend on the direct vote of the people, held at regular and frequent intervals. If the people wish to change the Government the simple remedy is to vote against it. In the event of an adverse vote the Crown, to which British Union is entirely loyal, will intervene, and H.M. the King, in the restoration of his full historic prerogative, will send for new ministers who in his opinion have a good chance of receiving the support of the country at a fresh vote. Thus in the permanent system of British Union nothing intervenes between Government and people. No log rolling in Parliament or intrigue in the lobby can shake the power of Government. The will of the people and that alone can make and break the Government.

Opposition Parties

But the "democrat" at this point usually expostulates that the people cannot decide to vote against a Government if no opposition parties exist organised for party warfare. Surely of all the insults which financial democracy offers to the intelligence of the electorate this is the gravest. Are we really to believe that a great people cannot make up their mind that they do not like a Government, and give a vote to that effect, without a lot of little politicians bawling in their ears that they do not like it, and asking them to vote for a dozen confused and contradictory policies. The suggestion that a great nation cannot live without professional politicians is an insult alike to their intelligence and their temper. Yet the "democratic politicians " who pretend that the people are capable, without such advice, of giving a decision on the broad issue of whether they want a Government or not, are at pains to defend the present system, which rests on the grotesque assumption that every elector understands every national question ranging from currency reform and naval strategy to the price of beer.

The facts are surely at complete variance with the pretensions of financial democracy. The people are perfectly competent to give a verdict on the general conduct of Government without any assistance from a bawling match of politicians. The elector also is perfectly competent to elect a Parliament to deal with the technical problems of the modern age, provided he votes within his own occupation on problems and for personnel that he thoroughly understands. But in plain terms of commonsense the engineer or the doctor finds it a bad joke for his particular problems to be settled by a vast majority of the electorate who have not the slightest acquaintance with those problems.

We are faced with the necessity of combining the right of the people to control and dismiss Government with serious discussion of highly complicated and diverse problems. The solution of British Union is to give the people direct control over Government by direct vote of the whole nation at regular intervals, when they will give their verdict on the general issue whether Government is good or bad, and, at the same time, to give them a separate occupational franchise for the election of a serious and modern Parliament on which Government will rely for the detailed consideration of modern problems.

With this solution we challenge the present system of financial democracy which in theory rests on the absurd assumption that everyone understands everything. In practice it results in such complete confusion that the great interests can govern under cover of the all-pervading smoke screen, and the great rogues of finance can get away with their booty, while the antics of the little kept politicians distract the attention of the people from reality.

A Government resting on the direct vote of the people and a Parliament elected by the informed vote of the people reconciles freedom with action and lays the foundation of the modern State.

The House of Lords

The present House of Lords can find no place in a modern system and will be abolished by British Union. It will be replaced by a new Second Chamber which reconciles British tradition with modern Government. That Chamber will represent the proved ability and experience of the nation. It will comprise industrial representatives from the National Council of Corporations, representatives of all the main religious denominations, representatives of education, representatives of the Services and men and women automatically appointed by their long occupation of positions of conspicuous service to the State. From such an assembly of personal experience and ability Government can draw great reserves of capacity for advice and constructive suggestion in all the multifarious variety of modern problems. This conception also carries out in modern form the original aim of the British Constitution. The House of

Lords was constructed to represent the industrial, cultural, and spiritual aspects of the national life. In those days agriculture was the only industry and the peers owned most of the land. Today agriculture is not the only industry and most peers have little to do with the land, while even the most ardent defender of the House of Lords will not claim that the peers are today the sole repositories of national culture.

The present House of Lords, therefore, no longer executes the original idea of the Constitution and is an anachronism. British Union will implement that original British tradition by giving to the Second Chamber a character really representative of the industrial, cultural and spiritual life of the nation. In the latter sphere it is only right that in an enlightened age the religious beliefs of all the main sections of our fellow citizens should be represented. In practice as well as in theory British Union believes in religious toleration, and that belief will be implemented by the representation of all denominations.

Freedom of the Individual - The Press

It remains to consider the effect on the individual of this structure of Government in terms of human freedom and the full individual life. If we accept the premise that economic freedom is the only true basis of individual freedom in modern conditions it must be agreed that effective power of action in Government is the prerequisite of individual freedom. For such power of action is necessary to bring to an end the economic chaos which today robs the individual of economic liberty in an age from which science can win this boon for all. But some still shrink from the only means of securing the larger economic liberty for the people through fear that the process will deprive them of a "political liberty" which in fact does not today exist. This type can find no answer in practical detail to the simple query, when have they ever got anything for which they have voted? They are baffled completely by the further question, what is the use of a "political liberty" which has never yet brought them any practical result? So they usually fall back on vague generalities concerning the inestimable boons of freedom of speech and freedom of the Press."

It is, therefore, necessary to examine in a little detail in what freedom of Press and speech today consists, and what would be the position of these "principles" under British Union Government. It may at once be stated categorically, to the surprise of many, that the freedom of the individual in these respects will be far greater than it is today. What freedom of the Press does the individual possess today? He certainly does not possess the freedom to secure the printing in the Press of either news or views which do not suit the interests of the Press. In the national Press, at any rate, he may not even humbly creep into back page correspondence columns if his opinions be regarded as in any way dangerous.

What prospect has the individual of founding a national newspaper of his own in conditions where monopoly has reached the point that no newcomer can hope to make good unless he can command millions of capital? A man of relatively moderate capital resources may possibly acquire control of a local paper of purely local influence or even, by a lifetime of hard work, may build such a modest influence in the State by genuine journalism without much capital resources. But no other save the great finance powers can now arrive in the national Press in modern monopoly conditions. So, in fact, when our opponents speak of the freedom of the Press they mean the power of the great financiers to purvey their opinions and their news to the people, with scant reference to the merits of the journalism, but with much reference to the weight of money power, which enables them to purchase circulations by canvass and free gifts, for which the advertisements of the great interests alone can recompense them.

The national Press, in fact, long since has become a matter not of journalism but of finance. In such circumstances what transparent mockery it is to tell the individual that he possesses freedom of opinion and of Press, for he, too, can start a newspaper. It is equivalent to the alleged statement of the classic Tory that Britain was a free country because rich or poor alike were free to sleep on the Embankment.

Free Speech

As for freedom of speech, in what today does it consist? It is true that anyone can carry a soap box to a street corner and from that eminence may make any moderate noise that he sees fit to emit, unless the whim of the local police chief transports him on charge of obstruction before a bench of magistrates selected for other political qualifications than street corner oratory. But may we not assume as the premise of the argument that none but a purely "mental" type desires to talk under these conditions purely for the sake of talking without any effective action following from his words? Judged by that criterion of reality, freedom of speech does not exist. For the persuasion of our countrymen is meaningless unless we can persuade them to do something. That power does not exist without a party machine to mobilise their votes, and party machines are not the possessions of individuals but of the great interests.

Freedom of speech for the individual is confined to the "mental" type who enjoys indefinitely a fruitless exercise of his lungs at a street corner without the slightest prospect of his words ever being translated into action. In fact, "freedom of speech" under financial democracy is merely another solemn make believe which obscures the reality of tyranny. No individual has any hope of producing any practical effect by words unless he serves one of the great party machines and, as we shall observe in the next chapter, the party machines in their turn serve the great interests and by the very nature of the system which they support are inevitably the servants of finance. So in actual practice under this system freedom of speech is the freedom to be the servant of the financier.

To this the retort may be made that any individual is free to win the support of his fellow countrymen, and in so doing from their enthusiasm to create his own machine in face of the money power. To that argument in turn we make the proud reply that this phenomenon has been achieved but once in post war Britain in the creation of British Union. And, the writer may add a note from that unique experience at the end of some years of such a struggle; if anyone believes that it is an easy and everyday task to create a new Movement from nothing by the force of the spirit alone in face of Money Power, Press power and Party power, he is welcome to the unparalleled exertion of that experience, but he will win success only at the cost of something in his own life and being that is not an everyday occasion.

Real Freedom of Press and Speech

In face of the present negation of freedom in the realm of Press and speech, British Union approaches a constructive solution in the determination to win real freedom of Press and speech for the people. That freedom will rest on two main principles: (1) that freedom of Press means the freedom of the people to read the truth in the national Press and not the freedom of finance power to tell lies to the people in support of vested interests; (2) that freedom of speech for the individual means an effective method of translating his opinion into action if by words he can persuade sufficient of his fellows to agree with him. In the sphere of the Press, therefore, we lay down the truly revolutionary principle that the Press shall tell the truth. To this end the proprietors of great newspapers will be liable to prosecution if it can be proved in Court that they have published news which is not true, and the penalty will be particularly severe if it can be shown that such Publication was deliberately and maliciously conceived in support of a private interest to the detriment of the national interest. It is a curious anomaly of present confusion that an individual who is libelled can obtain redress from the law but the nation when libelled can obtain no redress. Therefore, it will be open to a Government, elected by the people, on behalf of the nation to sue a newspaper proprietor if his paper publishes facts which are false to the detriment of the nation's interest, particularly if the object is to promote a private interest at the nation's expense. This will curtail the freedom of the Press to publish news which is untrue, but it will confer upon the people the freedom to read news which is true.

British Union takes the simple view that the freedom of the people to learn the truth should supersede the freedom of the vested interest to deceive the people. For this reason our new "freedom of the Press" rests on the simple but revolutionary principle that the Press shall tell the truth. Consequently neither national nor local paper which tells the truth will in any way be affected, and no proprietor can have any complaint unless he makes the unexpected admission that he is in the habit of not telling the truth in his papers at present.

Some organs of the national Press no doubt will pass unscathed through this test and certainly the great majority of our local papers. For local papers, on the whole, are straightforward purveyors of news, serving their localities as honest journalists who give a fair representation to all opinions, with a responsible regard to national interests.

If the whole national Press was conducted in the same method and in the same spirit as the majority of the local Press they would have nothing to fear from British Union Government.

Free Speech and Corporate Life

The machinery for putting into practice the principle of freedom of speech is equally definite. We start from the premise that if freedom of speech is to be a reality the individual must possess effective means of translating words into actions. To this end any individual with industry, interest, or profession, will be invited to enter into the appropriate Corporation, the detailed structure of which is suggested in Mr. Raven Thomson's able book on this subject and will not here be repeated beyond a survey of economic function in Chapter 4. Within the Corporation every one is not only permitted but by every means encouraged to express opinions both constructive and critical, and is provided with a means of making opinion effective. For if the individual can move the relevant Corporation by argument that Corporation's opinion, representing a very substantial factor in the State, is transmitted to Government, and for Government to ignore Corporate opinion would be to court dismissal at the next vote on universal franchise by the sum of individual voters who comprise the Corporations.

The mechanism of the Corporation, ready to the hand of the individual, is a more powerful instrument for the expression of free speech in effective terms of reality than the lonely and meaningless pedestal of the street corner orator. Through Corporate life the individual wins meaning and reality for freedom of speech. Such real and effective freedom of speech is a basic necessity for British Union Government which in the achievement of a revolution in national life must ever carry the people with it, and maintain a far closer contact with the people's opinion than Government possesses today.

It is good enough for the Governments of financial democracy to consult the people in a mock election once in five years in the hope that they will go to sleep in the interval so that Government can go to sleep as well. That is a procedure possible for Governments which in reality only exist to preserve the existing system and to guard its vested interests. But such a conception is not good enough for a revolutionary Movement determined to wrest from chaos a nobler civilisation. For such an achievement it is not enough to obtain the tacit consent of the people, it is necessary to carry the people with us all the way and all the time on the march to higher things. That is why we must know all the time what they are feeling and thinking and have precise means to that end. That is why we must devise machinery not only to give the people freedom of speech but to make that freedom effective. Contact between Government and people must ever be so close that the flame of our own revolutionary passion may pass continually from the souls of pioneers to fire and maintain the spirit of the people at a white heat of ardour unknown to the doped and tepid supporters of financial democracy.

For this shall be a great comradeship between the people and the Government they have elected to lead them. They must ever know what we are doing and we must ever know what they are thinking. That is why we believe in the people's real freedom of speech and will win it for them. Thus only can be secured that close and sacred union between the people and their Government by which alone a great nation shall march again to greatness.

Economic System – What Is Wrong ?

Economics of Poverty or Plenty

THE economic system is breaking down for reasons that are plain to see. But these reasons are never seriously discussed in Press or Parliament because the decadence of an economic System suits well the money power which controls Press and Parliament. Realisation by the people of the reasons for economic breakdown means the end of finance power. Therefore, every reason other than the plain and true reason must be provided, and every difficulty must be represented as temporary and transient rather than fundamental and inherent to a system in decline.

Every boom of the present system grows shorter and lesser; every depression grows deeper and longer. The crazy machine of the present economy rocks ever more violently toward a final disaster. The plain and simple reason is that the economic system is a century out of date. That system is the international system of trade and that system is responsible both for the evils and for the danger of the present time. In the sphere of economics, even more than in the sphere of Government, it should be clear that the method which grew from the facts of a century ago is not designed to meet the facts of today. The economic system was born of the age of poverty economics; we live in the age of plenty economics.

The facts are precisely the opposite to a century ago; yet the system in all fundamentals is precisely the same and the attitude of the parties is the same. To the international parties everything that has happened in the interval might never have occurred. The arrival of the technician, the introduction of the age of steam and later the age of power has altered for ever the economic environment of mankind. Yet all parties, including the Labour Party, support the international system of trade which preceded this vast revolution in fact and circumstance.

At the beginning of the international system the world was faced with the problem of poverty. Mankind could with difficulty produce enough to live. So it was argued with force by the economists of the period that each nation should produce what it was best fitted by nature to produce, judged by the sole criterion of cheapness, and should exchange such products with corresponding products from other nations. It was further argued that any barrier cutting across the thin trickle of international trade would universally diminish the standard of life, and in ensuing chaos might even result in the return of man to a primitive agricultural existence from which he had so recently struggled. It is unnecessary to discuss the merits of the arguments for or against that theory, though in retrospect we may condemn strongly the sacrifice of British agriculture to the extremes of that conception. It is redundant to discuss in modern times that theory because the whole premise on which it rested has been destroyed. It was born of the age of poverty, in which the question of the hour was how to produce enough to live.

This is the age of plenty, in which the question of the hour is how to sell what we can produce. The facts and the problem are exactly the opposite but the system and the parties remain the same. From all parties, platforms and Press we hear, in varying language and degree, insistence upon the maintenance and restoration of international trade and the free exchange of goods between nations. The main object of their denunciation is "economic nationalism," by which they mean any suggestion for nations themselves to produce as large a quantity as possible of the goods that they consume. Yet none can deny that every great nation today, with the aid of modern science, is itself capable of producing in almost unlimited quantity practically every commodity it requires, provided it has access to raw materials.

In face of all fact the politicians maintain a system that rests on the assumption that mankind can only with difficulty produce enough to live, and that goods must, therefore, be produced only by nations particularly suited to produce them and freely exchanged between nations. On the other hand, every technician and engineer knows that in modern conditions any great nation can turn out with mass production all essential commodities, provided it possesses skilled labour, machinery and raw materials.

In fact, the old parties all support a system resting on an assumption of facts which the thousands of technicians over whom they rule well know to be nonsense. Facts may change in gigantic revolutions of science but the politician changes never. This is not because he is so stupid as he appears but because, for a reason we shall study later, a system of decadence suits his masters better than a system which functions for the welfare of the people.

Export Trade

So our unfortunate industry is compelled to serve the international system and at all costs to national economy to fight for the export trade on which that system rests. In the battle for exports modern science and modern condition has again confronted our trade with an entirely new set of facts which have built such insuperable obstacles that the fight for exports ever since the war has been a steadily losing battle. The spread of modern science and technique has enabled our former customers to industrialise themselves. These new foreign industries are protected not by the obsolete weapon of tariffs but by barriers of complete exclusion which have not yet been lowered in response to the pious requests of British statesmanship, at innumerable international conferences, that these foreign nations should ruin their own industries in order to provide us with the markets that we lack. In remaining markets still open to us we are faced with a competition, unprecedented and irresistible, which has been created by the vile exploitation of modern science by finance power in the industrialisation of the Orient.

Western finance has provided the loans which have equipped the East with equal machinery to the West, and has hired the Western technician to teach the Oriental to perform the simplified tasks of mass production with modern mechanical technique at a third of the wages and for longer hours of monotonous toil that white labour can endure. The result has been a stream of sweated goods undercutting British products or the markets of the world. Their deadly effect can be observed in the cold statistics that show the decline of Lancashire and Yorkshire exports under the attack of rising Japanese exports and the vast increase in Indian sweated products.

Internationalism and the Standard of Life

Not only are we subject to the undercutting of sweated products in the markets of the world. In addition the blessings of the international system permit, despite all pretence at protection, great and increasing quantities of these goods even to invade our home market. British industry is not only being driven by new enemies and new weapons from our world position, but is being counter-attacked as well on the home and still more on the Empire market.

In such circumstances we ask the old parties a simple question that has never yet been answered. How can any international system, whether capitalist or Socialist, advance or even maintain the standard of life of our people? The international system of trade admittedly means the more or less free exchange of goods between nations. How can we raise or even maintain British wages in the face of competition from sweated labour supplied with the same machinery but paid a third of the wages and working for far longer hours? Whether industry be capitalist and owned by the unrestricted individual, or Socialist and owned by the State, how can it function in modern conditions if the system be international? This question is the epitaph of international Socialism, for it drives every thinking Socialist, together with men of all parties, who seriously study modern conditions, into the ranks of British Union, which organises industrial freedom within the insulated boundaries of an Empire economic system.

Purchasing Power

The construction of that system belongs to the next chapter, for the analysis of breakdown must be pursued further to a conclusion. We indict the international system as the root of present evils in the economic sphere. In view of the facts above recited the effect of the international system is plain to observe on the main problem of our day, which is the problem of "purchasing power." Few will deny that the industrial question today is how to sell what we produce. None can deny the truism that to sell one must find customers and, as foreign markets progressively close in the light of export figures over any substantial period, the home customer becomes ever more the outlet of industry. But the home customer is simply the British people, on whose purchasing power our industry is ever more dependent.

For the most part the purchasing power of the British people depends on the wages and salaries that they are paid. Here the effect of the international system on the central problem of purchasing power becomes obvious. The wages and salaries of the British people are held down far below the level which modern science and the potential of production could justify because their labour is subject to the undercutting competition of sweated labour on both foreign and home markets. Again we ask, how can British purchasing power be increased or even maintained in face of such competition? Yet internationalism condemns us to such competition and as a result, while foreign markets close, the purchasing power of the British people remains far inadequate to provide a home market capable of absorbing anything approaching the full production of British industry. The result is the tragic paradox of poverty and unemployment amid potential plenty.

Thousands even in the boom periods of this system, let alone the depressions, walk the streets in unemployment, and machines are idle which are capable of producing the goods that millions require but lack the power to buy. Internationalism, in fact, robs the British people of the power to buy the goods that the British people produce. In final frenzy of this system, with accompanying mumbo jumbo from the witch doctors of its economics, the people are even taught to believe that some mystic virtue resides in goods exported for foreign consumption, but that no good can come of the production of goods by Britons for the benefit of Britons.

Rationalisation

In economic result every blessing with which science now endows mankind becomes in practice a curse. The rationalisation of industry with higher wealth potential should be the greatest benefit of the period. In fact, it is dreaded by the people because it brings ever increasing unemployment with every increase in the power to produce. The reason again is plain to see because each increase in the power to produce goods is not accompanied by a corresponding increase in the power to consume goods. On the contrary, because internationalism restricts purchasing power rationalisation results in a lesser rather than a greater power to consume the wealth that it produces. Rationalisation enables industry either to produce more goods with the same amount of labour, or to produce the same amount of goods with less labour. Because the purchasing power of the people is held down by the unfair competition of the international system purchasing power cannot increase at the same time that rationalisation increases the power to produce. As a result only the same amount of goods as before can be produced after rationalisation, and they are produced with less labour. More are thrown, with loss of wages, on to the scrap heap of unemployment, and purchasing power is further diminished just at the moment it is essential that it should be increased if the victory of science is to be a blessing and not a curse.

Labour and Inflation

With the millstone of internationalism round their necks the old parties are incapable of dealing with the central problem of purchasing power. They are inhibited from the only solution of building up British wages to provide, by higher purchasing power, a greater market for British products, because higher wages are immediately undercut by cheap foreign competition and the industrialist who gives higher wages is put out of business. So Conservatism contents itself with a quiet drift to disaster in the hope that endless repetition of the the prosperity may by medieval incantation invoke prosperity. Labour, on the other hand, turns to remedies which make confusion worse confounded on the lines pursued by Mr. Leon Blum, the Jewish Socialist Prime Minister of France, who was hailed by Mr. Attlee as a model for the Labour Party just before he fell from power, leaving French economics in chaos. Because it is impossible for Labour genuinely to increase purchasing power in face of the sweated competition of the international system, which they support, they turn to the false creation of illusory purchasing power by the disastrous measure of inflation.

This process was well described in the City columns of Labour's organ, the "*Daily Herald*," in an eulogy of their other foreign hero, Mr. Roosevelt. "In modem conditions a reforming Government must maintain a constant stimulus of Government spending ... we have learnt, not that a reforming Government cannot make a system of partly private enterprise work, but that it cannot make it work today without a constantly inflationary pressure ... The mere pressure of unemployment and of falling Federal revenues will force a big budget deficit on the President."

So the once Socialist Party places its only hope in reformist doctrines which rest on the simple disaster of unbalanced budgets and inflation. This is the Nemesis of making great promises within the limits of a system that cannot deliver the goods. This is the fatality of supporting international Socialism in an age when only National Socialism can work. To inflate means to increase the supply of money without any corresponding increase in the supply of goods, and the result is on historic record in all countries that have tried it. Prices rising far more rapidly than wages diminish the real wages of the workers and create a speculators' paradise, with vast profits for the Stock Exchanges and rising cost of food and living to the people. Inflation and the opposite policy of deflation, which was pursued by the previous Labour Government, alike serve none but the financier who lives by flux and chaos. Inflation with a continually rising price level diminishes real wages and makes speculators' profits. Deflation by continually depressing the price level throws thousands into unemployment and increases the burden of all dead weight debt by making the fixed interest of the bond holder more valuable than it was before.

Each process serves the financiers alone; the first process was the policy of the last Labour Government and the second process would be the policy of the next. For Labour is prevented by an obsolete international creed from pursuing the only solution of building high British wages within a British economic system to enable the British people to consume what the British people produce. Any fool can inflate and appropriately enough this is the only remedy now left to the Labour Party.

They talk of "public works" and certainly public works of a useful and remunerative character should be undertaken by any vigorous Government to bridge the gulf between the breakdown of the present economic system and the creation of a new. The writer, when a Minister in the last Labour Government, planned such works with such an object on a great scale and pressed them without avail on that Government to the point of resignation. But public works undertaken in perpetuity without any serious intention of building a new economic system can have only one result. They pile up the burden of public debt which has to be supported from the declining revenue of a decaying system. This artificial attempt to supply a substitute for the purchasing power of the people in the end makes disaster worse, if indefinitely pursued as an alternative to the building of a new economic system. Public works, therefore, are only justified to bridge the gulf between the old and the new systems.

The Obsolescence of International Socialism

That Labour now has no serious intention of even attempting the building of a new system is all too clear. They are paralysed into ineffective and ever disastrous reformist doctrines by new and modern facts which their original theorists could not foresee, and the present leaders of Labour are incapable of fresh original thought.

The new facts which have destroyed the theory of international Socialism and in practice reduced it to an ineffective and disastrous reformism are plain to see. The first fact is the sweating of Eastern labour by Western finance to undercut the standards of the West. This event has already been examined and alone renders impossible international Socialism. The second fact is that international Socialism has always rested on the theory summarised in the slogan "workers of the world unite," and that after 80 years of this appeal the workers of the world are further than ever from unity. On the contrary, in the interval capitalism has got on with the task of introducing new and sweated workers who are incapable even of reading a Socialist manifesto. Therefore, all hope of freeing themselves from the consequences of internationalism by effective international action has completely faded. The third fact is that the evolutionary method of the Labour Party has become entirely unsuited to an age of revolutionary fact. In practice revolution by the method of evolution has proved a contradiction in terms. Facts move too fast for the Labour Party and the process of nationalising one or two industries and awaiting results before taking "the next step" becomes a farcical delusion in a period during which the whole economic system threatens to collapse about our ears.

While an economic system crashes the only contribution of Labour's evolutionary method is to nationalise one or two of the most obsolete industries, of course, with full compensation, as they always emphasise, to the dispossessed capitalist. So Labour is left holding the baby of decaying industry while the rogues of capitalism make merry with the proceeds of "compensation" in the decadence of a dying system, and the arms of Government are cluttered with their discarded and exhausted offspring. The "inevitability of gradualness" and nationalisation step by step with the hope of arriving at the Socialist State in the course of several generations have become doctrines too absurd to be tenable in the face of the modern electorate. So, at a loss for any effective plans of universal action which can only rest on the principle of power in Government, that in principle Labour denies, they tamely accept their Trade Union Leaders complete negation of Socialism which was summarised by Mr. Bevin's remarkable statement: "We must consider carefully the question how far the State should be permitted to interfere in the regulation of wages and conditions.

Our Movement is a voluntary one, and the claim for State regulation must not be carried too far. It might easily lead us on to the slippery slope of the totalitarian state" (Trade Union Congress, reported in "Manchester Guardian," 7/9/37). Their original theory thus entirely abandoned, Labour falls back in practice on the "reformist" doctrines of inflation after the model of Blum and Roosevelt. In so doing Labour performs its classic role and fulfils its historic destiny. For international Socialism is one of the chief instruments of chaos by which lives international finance.

In every sphere of national and world policy we find today international Socialism and international finance marching hand in hand. International Socialism creates, by weakness in Government and muddled folly in method, the flux and the chaos on which battens and thrives the financial parasite of the world.

Finance and Flux

By flux lives the financier and by flux dies the producer. The financier in the inner ring buys at the bottom and sells out at the top. To him, therefore, it is essential that a bottom and top should exist, or in other words that flux should exist. The producer, however, before all else requires stability. To him the greatest disaster is that the price level should be lower when he sells his goods than when he produces his goods. Yet this occurs in every depression of the system of flux by which the financier lives. The up and down of the economic system, in what are called booms and depressions, are poison to industry but the life blood of finance. Such fluctuation provides the normal business of finance, but in recent years greater and richer harvests have come its way in the sudden crash of currencies and economic systems. Before the pound was devalued in 1931 and the franc in 1937 it was a happy coincidence for the financiers that the respective Socialist Prime Ministers in Britain and France (old "model" MacDonald and new "model" Blum) should assure their nations that never, in any circumstances, would pound or franc be devalued. The interval during which the currencies were sustained by public belief in these statements enabled the financiers to get their money out of the country at a high rate of exchange, and later after devaluation to make enormous profits by bringing it back at a low rate of exchange.

Further fortune fell to the financiers towards the close of 1937, when the prosperity boosting of Conservative ministers gave such confidence to small investors that stock markets for the time held up fairly well, no doubt with the result that big financiers were able to unload on the public in a good market with a view later to buying back when prices touched bottom. But these are rare and refreshing prizes of finance apart from the normal business of profiting by the flux of the system.

Gambling in Commodities

To understand the present fate of the producer it is necessary to study how the flux of the international system is created. The flux of the system arises from the unlimited mobility of inter optional finance and the unlimited power to gamble in the primary commodities which supply the productive industries of the world. It is notable that each post war depression has been preceded by a large rise in the price of primary commodities, followed by a collapse in price. This is due for the most part to gambling by financiers in the raw materials that supply the industries of the world. The immense power of modern production responds immediately to boom demand by an increase in production which exceeds even boom demand. Glut is the result because even a boom of the present system is inadequate to absorb production by reason of the fact that the ultimate market of the people's purchasing power is insufficient. Therefore, glut arises in relation to effective demand and price collapse ensues, with all the familiar phenomena of depression. Finance greatly accentuates the chronic tendency to overproduction, born of under-consumption, by speculation, particularly in primary products, directly a boom increase in demand sets in motion a tendency to increasing price.

So the natural tendency of a system which lacks fundamental purchasing power, for reasons already examined, to produce glut and price collapse, is accentuated to the point of disaster by financial speculation which preys upon the deep-rooted disease of the system. The quick jumping financier is in on the rising market and out of the falling market with a fat profit, while the producers of the world are left to hold the baby in a market of falling prices. It is true that in longer and slower swing of the pendulum between boom and depression these factors would in any case arise in an international system which is inherently incapable of balancing the power of production by consumption. But the increasing and violent oscillations of the system, which today approaches collapse, are due to the financial parasite fastening on to the weak point of the international system and, like a microbe of disease, gravely aggravating a congenital weakness. Internationalism might muddle along a few years more albeit with great suffering to the mass of the people, but the financial microbe of decadence produces a fever which may before long prove fatal. By fever the financier lives but the body of industry perishes.

Wall Street Dictatorship

The same power of almost unlimited mobility of finance in practice subordinates completely the economy of Britain to the economy, or rather chaos, of a foreign country. Finance in the City of London is so interlocked with finance in Wall Street, New York, that in practice the City of London has become a sub-branch of Wall Street. Let anyone who doubts this study the immediate reaction on the London Stock Exchange of any movement on Wall Street. For London follows Wall Street entirely irrespective of British conditions. In recent years adverse movements on the London Stock Exchange have followed adverse movements on Wall Street even in face of good British trade reports. On the other hand, upward movements on the London Stock Exchange have followed an upswing on Wall Street, even in face of a disastrous British unemployment return the previous day. What matters to finance in the City of London is not what is happening in British industry, but what is happening in Wall Street, New York.

Therefore, as under the present system the City of London controls British industry, the life of this nation in the final analysis is controlled by a sub-branch of Wall Street finance. A British farmer may be deprived of his livelihood because a gamble in the Chicago Wheat Pit has produced a collapse in price. A prosperous British industry may suddenly be reduced to a standstill because Wall Street speculation in primary commodities has brought a subsequent fall on the Wall Street Stock Exchange with consequent fall in the City of London, and a downward swing of all prices into depression. Thousands of Britons may walk the streets in unemployment because some big rogue of finance on the other side of the world has gambled in the raw materials of industry.

In fact, the British craftsman will make less money by studying and perfecting his craft than by studying the symptoms of Wall Street. Ironic indeed is the tragedy of this dependence for a people which possesses within our own great heritage of Empire the means to produce every raw material and every commodity we require, not only in abundance but in complete independence of world supply or world speculation.

Finance Power Over Government

This same power of almost unlimited mobility which the international system confers upon finance affords it also almost unlimited power over Governments which support the international system. It is inherent in the system that capital and credit shall have power of movement from one country to another. The power of the financier as an individual to shift his fortune in and out of the country is entirely unrestricted. If these great mobile forces of finance are suddenly transferred from one country to another the exchange of the deserted country begins to collapse and financial panic ensues, which in turn is followed by the collapse of government. The mere threat of this manoeuvre broke the weak Labour Government in 1931, and the execution of this tactic immediately broke Leon Blum's Socialist Government in France shortly after it had been hailed as a "model" by the leader of the British Labour Party. Yet despite this experience the Labour Party dare not include in its programme even a reference to a restriction on the right of the great financiers to wield a power which at any time can break a Labour Government or any other Government. The reason is that the international system, which the Labour Party supports, is innately dependent on international finance. It relies on the financier to supply credit for the international transit and sale of goods and capital for the "promotion of export trade" by foreign loans. The supply of these facilities by the great finance houses makes utterly dependent upon them the whole system of international trade, and in turn renders dependent upon them any Government which supports that system of trade. The reason, therefore, is not far to see why no mention of the great finance houses of the City of London has ever appeared in any programme of the Labour Party. So far from proposing to restrict their masters, like the primitive savage they hold it impious even to mention the name of their God. Labour's financial proposals are confined to the meaningless gesture of nationalising the Bank of England, which for all practical purposes under any strong system of Government is nationalised already.

In simple fact the power of international finance is absolute over all the old parties, because the operation of the system which they support gives finance at any time the power to break them.

Foreign Lending - the Disaster of the System

When we analyse the power of finance over the old parties it is not difficult to see why a system is maintained which serves the financier alone, although it is destructive in modern conditions of every producer's interest, and is disastrous not only to the economy but to the integrity of the nation. Finance is the master of the parties, and finance forbids the building of a national system to meet modern facts and maintains an international system whose obsolescence provides the parasite of decadence with profit. Not only is that profit provided by speculation in the fever of the system which has already been examined. The traditional business of finance under the present system depends on the maintenance of internationalism and is admittedly brought to an end by the creation of an Empire system. That traditional business is foreign lending which we have earlier observed has equipped against us our foreign competitors all over the world, and in recent years has exploited the East to the threatened ruin of the West.

The only motive of foreign lending is to derive a higher rate of interest from the equipment of our competitors than from the equipment of British industry. That interest can only be drawn annually from foreign nations in the shape of gold, services, or goods. As few of them have either gold or services to offer the annual interest on foreign loans is derived almost entirely from the import of foreign goods. Consequently the business of finance depends on foreign imports, because without such imports it cannot draw usury from abroad. Therefore, the interest of finance conflicts directly with the interest of the producer, because imports from abroad are a necessity to finance but a disaster to the producer For it should further be noted that the entry of foreign goods representing interest on foreign loans is not balanced by any corresponding exports of British goods. They are tribute from one country to another in respect of a past transaction without any countervailing payment. In fact their economic effect is precisely the same as the payment of German reparations after the war, which represented tribute from one country to another, in respect of the past transaction of the war, without any balancing export. The effect on the economy of the recipient was then clearly observed and denounced by the international parties of the Left, who now affect to regard interest payments on foreign loans as an unmixed blessing. International Socialism had no use for foreign tribute which entered the national exchequer, but has every use for foreign tribute which enters the private pocket of high finance. The economic effect of either transaction is equally disastrous to British economy, but the Labour Party draws a distinction in favour of the private interest, which is one of the many curious paradoxes of contemporary politics.

Thus the part of international lending in our national economy is clear. It is firstly to supply backward nations with the means to undercut us in the markets of the world, and secondly to draw a high rate of usury from the transaction in the shape of cheap sweated goods, which enter the British market to the complete displacement of British labour because they are balanced by no form of export. Yet the extension of foreign lending has been laid before the country as the highest ambition of British industry in almost all Mr. Neville Chamberlain's annual orations to the Bankers' Dinner as Chancellor of the Exchequer, while the theory of foreign lending and the rights of foreign investors are eagerly championed by the Labour Party.

Behind this theory every influence of the Press and old world economists is also arrayed. British Union challenges, root and branch, the whole conception of foreign lending. We have already observed that the result is interest payment in the shape of foreign goods, which displaces British labour by sweated labour as surely as if thousands of Japanese were imported to Lancashire and Yorkshire to take British jobs. We will now examine the original effect of a foreign loan which means the permanent divorce of British wealth from British consumers for the benefit, or rather for the exploitation, of foreign countries. That wealth, as a capital sum, can never return to this country, for the repayment of the capital of all foreign loans in the shape of foreign goods would not merely disrupt industry like the payment of interest, but would completely shatter the British economic system. So foreign loans mean in practice the permanent consumption of British produced wealth by foreigners and the permanent loss of that wealth to the Britons who produced it.

Yet the whole conspiracy of politicians, Press and economists teaches the British people to believe that to send steel to a remote country to build a bridge over a far away river, and to send bicycles for savages to ride over the bridge, without any hope of repayment of this exported wealth, is a transaction of sound economy and finance. While to keep that steel at home to build British dwellings, and the bicycles at home for Britons to ride along well made roads, is a principle of wild cat finance. The greatest of all bluffs put over the British people is the loan-export bluff, for it has induced them to alienate from themselves forever an enormous proportion of the wealth they have produced by the genius of their technicians and the sweat of their workers. Late in the day they begin to see that the export of machines which they created, and taught the world to use, is today resulting in the equipment of sweated labour to undercut them on every market in the world. Finance, secure in the equipment of the

East by the effort of the West, cynically deserts the origin of its strength and wealth for fresh Oriental pastures, where the yield of usury from the sweated is greater than the return of interest from the civilised. So in the final frenzy of the system finance drives the West to produce the means of its own destruction, and, not content even with this classic business of the money power, our financial masters now make the primary commodities and raw materials which serve our stricken industries the subject of world gambles whose fluctuations create a chaos in which industry is prostrated. But internationalism and the parasite which drives it to destruction have gone too far; and today greed and folly bring their Nemesis in the threatened destruction of the body on which they prey. That body is the industry and life of Western Man.

British Union Economic System

BRITISH Union recognises the disintegration of the system and will not attempt to reform the system. The machine in modern conditions has broken and a new machine is required to meet modern fact. By this we do not mean that we shall ever destroy for the sake of destroying or uproot existing institutions merely because they now exist. That was the fallacy of international Socialism, which began with the theory of changing everything and ended with the practice of changing nothing. On the contrary, whatever is good we shall preserve and adapt to a new synthesis and harmony of the nation, while ruthlessly cutting away the dead wood of obsolescence and decadence. The essence of our economic creed is the realist facing of facts and the adoption, even more in practice than in theory, of the quickest means of securing the essentials of national reconstruction. To that end we seek to reconcile every motive of individual exertion with the welfare of the nation as a whole.

The interest of the nation transcends the interest of every faction, but, in recognising the over-riding interest of the community, the individual as a member of the nation secures his own ultimate advantage. Every great institution of our national and traditional life which is workable and can be adapted to new ends will be preserved and woven into a new national pattern and purpose.

Empire System

Above all, we are determined not wantonly to discard but to turn to high advantage the heritage won for our generation by the heroism and sacrifice of those who have gone before. The conjunction of the vast resources of our Empire with the genius of modern science can solve the problem of our age. We are no weak nation stripped of overseas possessions and denied access to raw materials, for our past has bequeathed as opportunity to the present one quarter of the surface of the globe. Therefore, in pride of our past and in confidence of our present abilities we turn to the Empire as the basis of our economic system. In so doing we ask what other alternative is open to our generation? what other means have we either of finding an outlet for our production in face of closing world markets, or of winning freedom from finance tyranny which rules through the obsolescence and decadence of the international system?

If we believe from the evidence of our eyes and of every present experience that internationalism is outworn and in continuance threatens the very life of our industrial system and national integrity, what alternative to that system can we discover except an Empire alternative? If the analysis of the last chapter be accepted, or even in part accepted we are driven to our own Empire as the only alternative to chaos and exploitation.

The only relevant question to the modern mind is whether or not the Empire can supply the modern alternative to the breakdown of the obsolete international system. Can an Empire system afford to our people not merely as good a material life as they possess today, but a higher standard of civilisation than the world has yet seen? To that question we return an unhesitating "yes," and prelude a detailed description of the system with the statement of certain facts which none has yet been found to deny.

1. Within these islands and the Empire are workers whose skill is second to none in the world.

2. Within these islands and the Empire we possess technicians and can produce machinery second to none in the world.

3. Within the Empire alone we possess practically every resource of raw material which industry can possibly require.

4. Within the Empire alone and with our own resources of men, machines, and raw materials, we can immensely increase our present wealth production, provided we have a market for which to produce.

These facts have not yet been challenged and, unless they can be disproved, it is possible to build in our Empire alone, without the need of any assistance from the outside world of chaos, a far higher standard of life than we possess today or than mankind has yet witnessed. But all depends on the condition of the last proposition stated above. Empire industry must have a market for which to produce and that is nothing else but the power of our people to consume. We have studied in the last chapter the factors which deprive the British people of the ability to consume the goods which they produce. Deliberately we build an Empire system that rests on the simple principle that the British people shall consume what the British people produce.

Home Market

The first act in the building of a new system is clearly to free the people of these islands from the forces which deprive them of purchasing power and to build a home market which rests on the high purchasing power of the people. High wages is a basic principle of our economic system, because high wages alone can give the people the power to consume the goods which they produce. The first factor which prevents high wages at present is the undercutting of British labour, even on the home market, by cheap foreign products often far below in price our present production costs

To this situation we apply the simple principle that nothing shall be imported into Britain which can be produced within Great Britain. The implementing of this principle means the exclusion from these islands of some £360 millions of manufactured and agricultural products which are now imported annually. To replace these by British products, on any current computation of production and employment, will give employment to nearly a million and a half of our people. In addition, British industry will be free on the home market from the cheap foreign competition which today holds down wages and diminishes the extent and purchasing power of the home market.

But British Union system for the home market does not end there for it would be idle to prevent the undercutting of British labour by sweated goods from abroad if we still permitted the undercutting of British labour by sweated goods produced at home. It is useless to protect our standard of life from the foreign employer who pays low wages if we still expose it to the attack of the British employer who pays low wages. To meet this situation British Union constitutes the Corporate system, and the effect of that system in preventing sweated production within Great Britain is plain and direct.

The first objective of the great industrial Corporations will be the elimination of sweated competition from within, when the Government, by exclusion, has eliminated sweated competition from without. They will lay down the minimum wage rate over the sphere of industry which they cover and infringement of these wage rates will be a criminal offence. But the function of the Corporations will be not merely static but dynamic. It will be their task progressively to adjust consumption to production power, and thus to overcome for the benefit of industry and people the problems created by rationalisation and our ever advancing industrial and mechanical technique. In other words, it will be the duty of the Corporations to raise wages and salaries over the whole sphere of industry as science and industrial technique increase the power to produce. Consequent on the elimination of sweated competition, both from without and from within, no limit will exist to the extent to which producing power can thus be increased except the limit set by scientific and productive advance.

When the purchasing power of our own people is so high that

their demand provides a market for the labour of every man and woman who wants a job, and for the full capacity of every machine, we must call a halt until further scientific achievement makes possible a further advance in the standard of life. For to increase purchasing power without a corresponding increase in the production of goods is to incur the disaster of inflation. On the other hand, an increase of purchasing power, accompanied by a planned advance in the production of goods, is not inflation but an increase in the production and consumption of real wealth. Thus we shall arrive at the point of true civilisation, when useful employment can be found for the whole population and for all machinery, and the main question of that future will be whether further to increase production or to reduce the hours of labour. For the final solution of the present problem which is miscalled "overproduction" is both to increase wages and to reduce the hours of labour, thus at last making man the master of machine instead of the machine the master of man.

Position of Individual Firms - Tory Protection

We seek to build a home market in which the British can consume what the British produce by the joint method of excluding sweated products from without and the prohibition of sweated production from within. The relative position of individual firms will remain the same on the new high wage basis as on the present low wage basis. If you compel A to raise wages but permit his rival B to maintain low wages the only effect is to put A out of business by giving an advantage to his rival B. But if you compel both A and B to raise wages their relative competitive position remains the same. Under British Union system any individual is free to put his rival out of business by greater efficiency than his rival, but he is not free to put his rival out of business by paying lower wages. The essential difference between the economic "insulation" of British Union policy and any protective proposals ever advanced by the Conservative Party can thus easily be discerned. We will assume, for the sake of argument, that the incredible happened and that the Conservative Party gave to industry the real protection from foreign competition which they have always promised at elections, in glaring contradiction of their practice when they recently possessed record majorities in Government and yet permitted the annual import into these islands of £360 millions of foreign manufactures and agricultural products. If the miracle occurred and Conservative pledges were actually carried out this vital difference would exist between their policy even in this regard and that of British Union. Behind their protective barrier no organisation would exist to prevent the production of sweated goods and unfair undercutting by low wages of one British firm by another.

Conservative rejection of the Corporate system deprives them of any means to this end. Consequently, despite their protection, British wages would still be kept down by sweated competition from within even if they had eliminated sweated competition from without. A further evil undoubtedly would arise under this unregulated and anarchic system which provides freedom only for the exploiter to exploit. Freed from all check and threat of foreign competition under Conservative protection the present tendency towards trust, combine and monopoly would greatly accelerate. Even more combines would come together to exploit the protected market without any let or hindrance. The classic tendency of the monopoly would quickly emerge in the increase of price to the consumer and the decrease of wage to the worker. Consequently protection unaccompanied by organisation and power in Government is an unmitigated evil. On the other hand, insulation from world chaos is the first and necessary action in the building of an economic system which can only thrive and advance in the high purchasing power of the mass of the people.

Imports, Exports and Empire

Thus British Union builds a home market capable of absorbing the maximum production of British industry, subject only to the necessity of acquiring outside these islands what we cannot here produce. At this point we turn to our own Empire overseas to secure the raw materials and some foodstuffs which Great Britain cannot produce. We shall offer to our Dominions and Colonies the direct bargain for which they have always asked. We will buy from them raw materials and any foodstuffs which we cannot produce here on condition that they accept an equivalent value of our manufactures in return. They are primarily producers of raw materials and foodstuffs and we are now primarily producers of manufactures and exports such as coal. A natural balance of Empire economy exists which policy in this country has done much to destroy by preferring to buy essential raw materials and food from foreign countries. As a result the Dominions have already been driven to the development of secondary manufacturing industries. That process, if long continued, may develop in the Dominions an economic self-sufficiency which may lead in time to their complete inability to accept our exports. Great Britain will then be faced with the retribution of internationalism in dependence on foreign supply, for which she can only pay by exporting goods to foreign markets that are rapidly closing against her. In fact, continuance in the policy of preferring the foreign to the Empire supply of raw materials and certain foodstuffs might finally spell the doom of these crowded islands when, in the future, they seek outside supplies for which they cannot make payment either in foreign or Empire markets.

On the other hand, an early development of Empire economic system can arrest the drift to this catastrophe. The process of developing secondary industries in Dominions and Colonies has not yet gone far enough to prevent a balanced Imperial economy. They offer to us still the simple bargain of their raw materials to be balanced by their acceptance of our manufactured exports in a £1 to £1 equivalent.

Why are the international parties, Conservative and Labour alike, so mad as to refuse? The answer to this riddle may be found in the deliberate maintenance of the adverse balance of payments under the existing foreign trade pacts, which should provide a conclusive argument for the abrogation of these pacts in favour of a balanced Empire trade. Under almost every foreign trade pact Britain imports more than she exports in return. The adverse balance of goods received represents interest payments made on past loans without any balancing export in return as described in the last chapter. So Great Britain refuses Empire trade and maintains the adverse balance of trade pacts with foreign nations for the sole reason that the process is a means of collecting the usury of the City of London.

An Empire system is sacrificed and we drift towards the disaster of dependence on an ultimate world system, in which we can find no means of payment for necessary imports, solely because the British Government and our economic system are debt collectors for the City of London. Not only must British labour be displaced in the home market by the import of sweated goods as interest payment, but we are forbidden to develop our heritage in an Empire economy because the millstone of foreign lending is still around our necks. We have to choose between an insulated Empire system, containing within its free boundaries the highest standard of civilisation that the world has yet seen, and the maintenance of a world usury system which in every sphere destroys the productive interest and oppresses the people. We have to choose between Empire and Usury; British Union chooses Empire.

Empire Development

It is clear that our system depends on the intensive development of an Empire which is today producing only a fraction of what it could produce. The question is sometimes asked whether we can rely on the co-operation of the self-governing Dominions with whose self-governing status we have no desire in any way to interfere. The question does not arise in the case of the Crown Colonies, because their control changes with the Government of Britain. In the case of the Dominions it surely follows that they will co-operate in the policy for which they have always asked. It is they who have demanded a market for their raw materials and for such foodstuffs as we could not produce in this country, and it is the Government of Britain who have refused in order to accept goods from foreign countries for reasons above stated. It is inconceivable, therefore, that the Dominions for any political reason should refuse a policy for which they have always asked and that offers to them such an advantage. If any Dominion Government for any purpose of political spite adopted such a course we would rely with complete confidence on the Dominion producer at an early election to sweep them from power, for he would not tolerate the sacrifice of his economic interests to any political prejudice. Our appeal for Dominion cooperation is based not only on kinship and history, but on an overriding mutual economic interest.

In the case of the Crown Colonies we affirm frankly that what has been won by the heroism of the British people shall be used for the benefit of the British people. Instruments like the Congo Basin Treaty, which are supported by the Conservative Party and make our African possessions the dumping ground of the world, will be repudiated, and British possessions will be preserved as a British market, with a result in itself, that current statistics prove, will go far to restoring our export trade. The great British colonial tradition of good and fair treatment of native populations will be preserved, but we shall challenge the illusion that backward and illiterate populations are fit for self-government when obviously they are not. Nor do we admit that the Western nations should be confronted with closed areas in the supposed interests of native populations, which have done nothing to develop their own territory before the genius of the Western mind and energy put them on the map of the world.

If "Left" theories in this sphere were logically applied America would be handed back to the original Red Indian inhabitants, and the white man would be barred from the land which his talent has created. In practice these high-sounding theories of native self-determination have resulted in no higher reality than the ruthless sweating and exploitation of native populations by

Western finance capitalists for the undercutting of the Western standard of life. In practice native "rights" have been the right to be exploited. Such exploitation of backward populations will be absolutely forbidden in British Union Empire, and as a result the poison stream of sweated goods will no longer enter the arteries from within the body of Empire. Good and fair treatment of native populations is a British tradition, but to stultify the white man's genius in order to preserve native "rights" to neglect fertile areas of the globe, or native "rights" to be exploited by finance capitalists for the destruction of the West, is an historic absurdity and a British tragedy. Therefore, consciously and determinedly we develop for the benefit of the British people the territory which the energy of the British people has made their own.

Agriculture

In developing the territory of our Empire British Union policy by no means forgets the development of our own native soil. The measures already described will not only save agriculture, but are the only measures that can save British agriculture. For our policy meets the two factors which today destroy agriculture and depopulate our countryside. They are (1) the flood of foreign imports, (2) the low purchasing power of our British people which deprives them of the ability to buy good British food.

By present conditions a conflict has been created between town and country in which the countryside has always been worsted since the Conservative Party ceased to be the party of the land and became instead the party of high finance. The farmer must have a better price in order to live and to pay his farm workers the decent wages that he would like to pay if prices permitted. Financial democracy meets his demand with the fact that under the present system the town workers, who are the bulk of the population, are too poor to pay a better price. So agriculture perishes, and the people are uprooted from the soil, with results to whose fatality all history bears witness. British Union policy resolves the conflict between town and country and welds their interests in a new national harmony. Every attempt to solve the agricultural problem in isolation from the national problem as a whole has failed, and will always fail.

British Union overcomes the dilemma of the countryside : (1) By raising the purchasing power of the mass of the people to the point that modern science permits by means already described; (2) By prohibiting entirely the import into Britain of any foodstuffs that can be produced within Great Britain. This policy preserves for British agriculture the home market and provides a market capable of paying for British products. In practice no substantial increase of price to the consumer need be anticipated, and in any event, the general increase in wages and conditions under a modern system will be far greater than any increase in farming prices. The farmer can increase production for an assured market without any very great increase of his present overhead charges. Consequently an increase in production without a commensurate increase in production costs will tend to prevent prices from rising. Yet greater production for an assured market will afford the farmer profit instead of loss, and the labourer a living in place of a starvation wage. In addition a Distributive Corporation will cut our redundant distribution costs and bring farmer and consumer closer together in the absence of a host of unnecessary middlemen who now take their toll of farmer and consumer alike. Measures to prevent profiteering in food are overdue, and if necessary, will be severe. But the basic guarantee of prosperity to British agriculture is the high purchasing power of the British people and that great home market is the constant aim of British Union policy. A market that is capable of paying for British food products can easily be preserved for British agriculture, because if the townsmen can pay for British food they will always prefer it as they know it to be the best.

More British Food

So British Union policy deliberately excludes from these islands all foodstuffs that can be produced within them. This will entail the production of another £200 million of British foodstuffs each year to replace foreign imports that will be excluded. The writer, in addressing hundreds of farmers' meetings throughout the land, has never yet found a farmer to deny that it is possible, provided they have an assured market for which to produce. Clearly it will take some years to evoke the maximum of British production.

In practical method Government will meet the Farmers' Union, which will have an even greater status within the Corporate State, and will inquire by how much British production can be increased in each succeeding year. Government will then undertake to cut down foreign imports by a corresponding amount until, at the end of a specified period, British production has entirely taken the place of the foreign import. The end will then be secured of a market for the full production of British agriculture which rests on the high purchasing power of the British people.

It is true that we cannot here produce all the diverse kinds of foodstuffs that we require. But like our raw materials we can acquire all the outside foodstuffs we need from our own Dominions and Colonies. In a choice between British and Dominion products the British must always come first, but plenty of room will still exist on British markets for Dominion foodstuffs. We now import annually £180 million worth of foodstuffs from the Dominions, and it is possible to increase British production by £200 million a year at the expense of the foreigner alone, without touching Dominion imports. Further, any cut in any particular branch of Dominion imports which it is necessary to make in the interests of British farming will be far more than compensated by the much greater demand of the British people for other Dominion and Colonial products, and raw materials, when our purchasing power is increased. British and Dominion production will divide between them a greatly increased British market on the principle of Britain First, Dominions and Colonies second, and the foreigner nowhere.

Foreign Food Prices

The absence of the foreign food product from the British market is a distressing thought to those international parties, Conservative and Labour alike, who have taught the people that to buy abroad is to buy cheap. But the people are no longer impressed, for they have found in fact that to buy abroad is to buy dear. In all recent sudden rises in food prices the rise in price of the foreign has greatly exceeded the rise in price of the British product. The reason is that the combine and monopoly have invaded also the control of the people's food. Immediately a tendency to price rise occurs the foreign monopolies rush up the price of food to the British consumer. If the international parties were allowed to carry the financier's game much further, and the British consumer by the ruin of British farming became completely at the mercy of foreign supply, the British people would find that to buy abroad from the foreign food combines was the dearest folly that they had ever committed.

The import of foreign foodstuffs is pursued as a sacred rite of the financial democratic system because those imports more than any other pay the interest on foreign loans as previously described. But as ever in decadence parasite grows on parasite, and today the policy of foreign food combines is to undercut and put the British farmer out of business in order that they may have the British consumer completely at their mercy. This crime has been permitted and encouraged by Conservative Governments which have given to the British farmer the "Board" and to the foreign combine the "Market."

Organisation for a market which does not exist is in any case without purpose. The old parties have merely given to the farmer restriction when all he needed was opportunity. The British farmer may be trusted to carry on his own business once he has a market for which to produce. He must be freed from the foreign import which destroys him, and the redundant middleman who exploits him, to serve a market which is capable of paying him a living. This Government can do this for farming and more, for every method of modern science and organisation to help the farmer in his task must be made available to British agriculture. British Union knows that no people can live that is uprooted from the soil and that the universal urbanisation of a population spells a doom inevitable and historic. British Union knows too that the men who carried British genius and the glory of our name and our achievement to the far corners of the earth, had roots deep in the soil of our native land. The little men and the little parties in the service of an alien finance have tried to sever the roots of the oak. We who come from the soil of Britain say that the oak shall stand.

The People's State - A Classless System

Heredity

THE system of British Union provides no place for the parasite. It has neither privilege nor place for those who seek to live on the efforts of others without giving anything in return. But the people's state has opportunity and place for all who serve the nation in an infinite variety of capacity. So British Union system of heredity is accordingly designed on the one hand to encourage to the utmost the initiative and enterprise of the individual not only in working for himself but also in deep and human motive in working for his children. On the other hand, it is devised to eliminate the parasite and to deprive of all hereditary advantage those who prove unworthy of their forebears' exertions and unworthy of the new nation. Therefore, a man, or woman, may by energy and enterprise not only enrich themselves but bequeath the result of their efforts to their children. But the children, either in industrial service or in public service, must render a service equivalent to the benefit they receive, or in default will lose their hereditary advantage in whole or in part. Equity Tribunals of People's Justice will be established to determine on commonsense lines such questions, which will be no more difficult to settle than many questions of equity that come before the courts today. The system will be woven quite naturally and easily into a general codification and simplification of the law of the land, in language which anyone can understand without dependence on a lawyer's racket.

The Land

Opportunities for public service on a far greater scale than exists today will be provided by the immense development in the social life of the new nation, which will call for leadership and effort in many spheres now closed. For one example, a real local leadership will again be required in a revitalised countryside. The original owners of the land in most cases gave such leadership until death duties and the victory of urbanism broke the system. They will again have such opportunity in British Union system, which seeks consciously the continuity of a stock with roots in the soil, and will accordingly lift from the land death duties and other burdens in return for real service to the land. But the landlord whose time, money, and energy are not spent among his own people in local leadership but are divided between a London night club and a continental resort will be ruthlessly dispossessed without any compensation. The land thus acquired by the State will be used for the development of owner occupier farms, and a mixed system of local leadership and owner occupier will result which will preserve the best traditions of the land and afford the maximum stability.

To the urban landlord British Union applies the same principle as to any other monopolist. Any attempt to exploit a shortage of any commodity by increasing the price to the people will be rigorously suppressed. So all rents will be controlled by law while any shortage of housing exists. As for the slum landlord he will simply be dispossessed without compensation and prosecuted like any other purveyor of commodities which are a danger to health. The landlord who without effort of his own seeks to take advantage of community effort by increasing the price of land in the neighbourhood of an expanding town or industry will be confronted by a simple dilemma. He will be taxed on his own valuation of the land, but the State will have power to acquire it at that valuation. If he assesses the value at a high figure he will be taxed at a high figure, and if he assesses it at a low figure he will be bought out at that figure with increment to the nation. Thus British Union will solve the ancient problem of "land values" by measures which place the land in the same category as any other potential monopoly. In practice, however, most ownership of urban land will pass to the State as that category of landlord is a great deal less likely than the leader of the countryside to justify his hereditary wealth by public service. It is unfair to discriminate between the land and any other form of hereditary wealth, but he who lives on the land without service to the nation will pass with other parasites.

Class

Liberal Socialism has ever striven to represent that only one form of hereditary wealth led to vicious results, namely the land in which their leading figures happened to have no interest. In fact, the worse vices of the hereditary system which British Union will sweep away arise from the transmission of hereditary wealth by quickly rich financiers and speculators, whose children have no sense whatever of hereditary responsibility in return for hereditary wealth. To such as these the "trustee of the nation" principle of all wealth owners under British Union are utterly lacking. From them, in particular, has come the disgusting spectacle of flaunting extravagance and paraded riches in face of poverty, which evoked from British Union the principle that "none shall stuff while others starve." Above all they have created the fatal distinctions of social class which British Union is determined to remove for ever. Their class values are based on money value and on nothing else. The accident of birth and the mere fact of being their "father's son" is held by these miserable specimens of modern degeneracy to elevate them without effort of their own above their fellow men. Not only are they given opportunity by their forebears's exertion, but many of them neglect that opportunity for any other end than the idle pursuit of pleasure, while they cumber the directorates of their hereditary businesses which underpaid technicians conduct. Here we see the apotheosis of the parasite deriving his snobbery from his father's efforts and marking the values of the snob by the capacity to squander in face of the starving. The snob and the parasite shall go, and with him shall go his values in the classless state which accords "opportunity to all but privilege to none."

Function

Class based on social snobbery and the accident of inheritance shall go. But British Union will not fall into the opposite stupidity of an unworkable equalitarianism which refuses to recognise between man and man or woman and woman any difference of function. A man shall be valued by what he is and not by what his father was. If he performs high service to the nation in the exercise of exceptional capacity he shall have fitting reward and status. To work, not only for money for self and children, but for position and honour among fellow men is no small and unworthy motive of mankind, and is a deep mainspring of human conduct which it is folly to ignore. The award of honour as the reward of money may go to great service and may be transmitted to children, but like hereditary wealth will be liable to removal if the children are unworthy.

To argue that all men are the same and that exceptional effort is worthy of no recognition is an error that robs of motive power important human enterprises. It is true that the great lights of humanity have illumined the path of mankind from no other motive than the inner light. But it is folly to ignore the fact that the overwhelming majority who achieve anything are moved by simple terms of honourable distinction and the winning of security for home and children. It is still greater folly to presume that all men are equally gifted in mind, muscle, or spirit; from that fallacy arises the fatal tendency of the present phase to slow down the pace of the fastest to that of the slowest. This grotesque assumption, if carried to its logical conclusion, would merely deprive the nation of the full exertion of exceptional ability by which alone great affairs can be conducted.

Education

The true solution is to eliminate the parasite of heredity but to give the utmost opportunity to talent wherever it can be found. Whether a man starts in castle or cottage he shall have equal opportunity to rise to the top and to use his talent if he possesses the capacity. This principle involves a complete revision of the present educational system, which largely confines opportunity to the accident of wealth. In the reconstruction of national education it will be also the deliberate aim of British Union finally to eliminate the last trace of class and snobbery.

Preliminary education will afford to all the same sound basis of classless and national education, subject to the right of all parents to secure for their children the religious atmosphere they desire. But later education will differentiate widely, not on the principle of wealth but purely on the principle of talent. At present the children of the rich are normally educated at least until eighteen years of age, altogether irrespective of their capacity for education. The children of the poor, on the other hand, are largely thrust into industry at the age of fourteen, irrespective of talent for the higher education which is denied. It will be the policy of British Union to continue the education of all by varying methods and degree until eighteen years of age. In the present low standard of life to deprive parents of the small wages of children who displace their elders from industry would be a hardship. In the higher standard of life which science will produce within a modern system adults will earn enough to keep the home together without dependence on the wage pittances of children.

Therefore British Union will render it possible to continue education for all until an age when they can be regarded as truly adult and ready to enter industrial life. But from the age of fifteen onwards education will be sharply and progressively differentiated between varying degrees of talent.

All children of outstanding ability will have open to them by progressive selection a straight road from cradle to university. The opportunity open to every child will be the same, and the same path to higher education will be available to all talent. Those on the other hand who cannot benefit beyond a certain point from the absorption of academic knowledge, as a preliminary to the practical in life, will undergo different forms of education and training, and at an earlier age will specialise for some definite avocation. Above all, every child, of whatever talent or capacity, will receive a sound physical and nutritional basis for the struggle of life. The care of the child is the special care of British Union, for British Union will be not only the nation's trustee of today but also of tomorrow. That infinite morrow of British destiny depends on building a nation with physique and morale adequate to the immense duty of British leadership. In that high purpose we guard the child.

True Patriotism

The people's state of British Union thus secures the principle of opportunity for all but privilege to none. Every Briton shall have equal opportunity in the land of his birth, and, therefore, equal possession and love of that land. Thus shall be born the true patriotism which is determination to build a land worthy of a patriot's love. This is something very different from Conservatism's exploitation of that profound emotion to guard the vested interests which possess Britain today. No wonder that so many of the dispossessed reply to the "Tory patriot" that "it is your land, not our land, that you ask us to defend." Britain looks different to the "father's son" arriving at a night club door in a Rolls Royce than to the man of possibly greater capacity and, in the war at least, of greater service, who is shivering in the rain or fog of a country that has used him and discarded him. In British Union our land will look the same to all, for it will afford to all the same opportunity and so will belong to all.

Today patriotism and progress are divided by the parties into opposing camps when, in fact, they should be indissolubly united. Love of country has been exploited by reaction and hatred of country has been exploited by those who masquerade in the clothes of progress. In reality patriotism dies without progress because the continual advance of man alone can build a country worthy of love. On the other hand, progress dies without patriotism because the first object of progress must be the elevation of the native land, and care for every country but their own has robbed the misnamed parties of progress of all appeal to the enthusiasm and effort of their fellow countrymen. We love our country and we love our people, and for that reason we stand both for patriotism and for progress in the union of two great principles which the war of the parties has divided. The National Socialist creed of British Union says to our countrymen "if you love our country you are National, and if you love our people you are Socialist." We ask patriots to join with us in building a country worthy of a patriot's love, in which the class distinction of the snob and the privilege of the parasite shall exist no more. But in place of class and privilege shall arise the brotherhood of the British to give equal opportunity to all in service and possession of their native land.

The Jewish Question

THE Jewish question should receive proper space in relation to national affairs in any book which deals with the modern problem. This question was no concern of our Movement at the outset, but the Jews themselves very quickly made it a concern. We advanced for the consideration of our countrymen the policy which appears in these pages, without raising any racial question or troubling with any faction. Long before we raised the Jewish question in any form, however, that question was forced on our attention.

The evidence for this statement can be ascertained by any one from police court records. For the inquirer will learn that of those convicted for physical attacks on Blackshirts 50 per cent were undeniably Jewish in the six months which preceded the introduction of this question by the British Union in October,

1934. Our organisation had then been in existence two years and we had observed that, in addition to an extraordinary proportion of Jews in the physical assailants of our members (when out numbered), the victimisation of our people by Jewish employers and the pressure of Jewish interests on our supporters was a very distinctive feature of our struggle. This occurrence forced the Jewish question on the attention of many who had paid no more attention to Jews or their particular problem and character than to any other section of the community.

The resultant study revealed a fact not difficult to ascertain, that a remarkable proportion of Jews were engaged in practices which the system we proposed would bring to an end. Throughout the ages Jews have taken a leading part in international usury and all forms of finance and money lending, while smaller exemplars of the method have engaged in such practices as price cutting, the sweating of labour, and other means of livelihood which any ordered and regulated economy must bring to an end. So the reason was not far to seek why we had incurred the bitter and especial enmity of Jewish interests.

Some say that it is a wicked animal that defends itself when attacked, but the response of the Englishman to a blow in the face is traditional. That response was greeted immediately by all the organs which Jewish interests control with a loud clamour of racial persecution. It is well, therefore, to set down exactly what we propose on this question, and the reader may decide for himself whether this policy is persecution or simple justice which is necessary to the integrity of our own nation.

Rights of the State

We do not attack Jews on account of their religion, for our principle is complete religious toleration, and we certainly do not wish to persecute them on account of their race, for we dedicate ourselves to service of an Empire which contains many different races and any suggestion of racial persecution would be detrimental to the Empire we serve. Our quarrel with the Jewish interests is that they have constituted themselves a state within the nation, and have set the interests of their co-racialists at home and abroad above the interest of the British State.

An outstanding example of this conduct is the persistent attempt of many Jewish interests to provoke the world disaster of another war between Britain and Germany, not this time in any British quarrel, but purely in a Jewish quarrel.

None can argue that it is a principle of racial or religious persecution for a State to lay down the principle that its citizens must own first allegiance to the nation of which they are members and not to any faction at home or abroad. That many Jews regard themselves first as members of Jewry and secondly as British citizens is not only a matter of simple observation but of proof from Jewish literature and statement. British Union, therefore, affirms the simple principle that Jews who have placed the interests of Jewry before those of Britain must leave Great Britain. In particular, those who have indulged in practices alien to British character and tradition must leave these shores. Those against whom no such charge rests will not be persecuted, but will be treated as the majority of their people have elected to be treated. They have maintained themselves as foreigners in our midst and as such they will regarded, without the privileges of the British citizenship which to them has been a secondary consideration.

We British have not been in the habit of persecuting foreigners and we shall not in British Union develop that habit. On the contrary, we have a tradition of according good treatment to foreigners who have particularly served this nation and any such Jews have certainly no reason to anticipate any breach of this tradition. But all nations have a right to say that foreigners who have abused their hospitality shall leave the country, and any State has a right to affirm that all citizens shall own allegiance to the nation and not to any external power.

It remains to inquire whether in fact it is fair to regard the Jew as a foreigner. The simple answer is that he comes from the Orient and physically, mentally and spiritually, is more alien to us than any Western nation. If a community of several hundred thousand Frenchmen, Germans, Italians or Russians were dumped in our midst they would create a grave national problem. That problem would be particularly grave if they maintained themselves as a community in our midst, owning spiritual allegiance to their original nation, and indulging in methods and practices altogether alien to British character and temperament. Such an event would create a problem so serious that a solution would have to be found. Yet the Jew is more remote from British character than any German or Frenchman, for they are Westerners and the Jews are Orientals.

The Final Solution

This problem has been raised with increasing pressure in most European countries in the inevitable opportunity presented to Jewish method by the "decline of the West." It has become a European question of first class magnitude in which Britain must offer leadership in accord with British tradition. It is not in accord with British character to keep Jews here in order to bully them - that we will never do. On the contrary, the statesmanship of the future must find a solution of this question on the lines of the Jews again becoming an integral nation.

There are many waste places of the earth possessing great potential fertility, and the collective wisdom of a new Europe should be capable of finding territory where the Jews may escape the curse of no nationality and may again acquire the status and opportunity of nationhood. It is true that Palestine is not available as a home for the Jewish race throughout the world, for the simple reason that it is already the home of the Arabs. Whatever wrongs the Jews are alleged to have suffered will not be righted by the crime of inflicting with violence far greater wrongs on the Arab ally who trusted the word of Britain in war.

The most that the Jews can reasonably hope from Palestine is respect for their holy places and free access to visit them as the pilgrim Arab has access to Mecca. Other territory must and can be found for the solution of the Jewish problem of the world. Is it really persecution of the Jews to suggest that they should again become a nation in suitable territory? If so, it is persecution which has been acclaimed by the prophets and seers of Jewry as the final objective of their race for the last two thousand years. Their leaders have always proclaimed the wish of Jewry to become again a nation. Why is it persecution to say "very well, you shall become again a nation"? It is not persecution unless it be true that every protestation of Jewry in this regard was hypocrisy throughout the ages, and that their real desire was not to reunite their scattered race in national dignity but to become for ever the parasite of humanity.

If, therefore, Jewish declarations be sincere, the effort of European statesmanship to find a solution of this problem by the creation of a Jewish National State should not be resisted by Jewry. The only thing the Jews cannot ask in the name of justice and humanity is that Britain should found for them that state in blood by the slaughter of Arabs and the rape of their homes.

In summary of our policy on this question we affirm the right of every nation to deport any foreigner who has abused its hospitality, and we hold the aim of finding, together with other European nations, a final solution of this vexed question by the creation of a Jewish National State, in full accord with the age-long prayers of the prophets and leaders of the Jewish race. Is this persecution or is it justice?

British Foreign Policy

The International of Finance and Socialism

BRITISH foreign policy should hold two objectives: (1) the maintenance of British interest; (2) the maintenance of world peace. These two objectives do not conflict but coincide. British Unions deep quarrel with the virtually unanimous policy of the old parties is that it has sacrificed both the interests of Britain and of world peace to a political vendetta. Particularly we denounce the pursuit of that feud to the risk of British lives and world catastrophe because it is dictated by subservience to the vile international interests which command the old parties.

In this sphere international finance and international Socialism march openly hand in hand. They are by nature complementary forces of disaster, for the policy of international Socialism creates the flux and chaos by which finance lives and the producer perishes. Still more, in foreign policy their community of aim and of method should be clear to all, together with the reason of their unholy union. Certain countries have at once extirpated the control of international finance and the hopes of international Socialism. No reason exists in British interest to quarrel with these countries and every reason of world peace forbids the quarrel. Yet the feud of international finance and its twin, international Socialism, thrusts the manhood of Britain toward mortal quarrel with these nations.

Germany and Italy, despite a present poverty of natural resources have, at least, broken the control of international finance, and Germany in particular has offended this world power by summary dealing with the Jewish masters of usury. So every force of the money power throughout the world has been mobilised to crush them, and that power does not stop short at payment for its vendetta in British blood. Any study of the Press and propaganda organs controlled by finance power can reach no other conclusion if we ask the simple question, what single interest of Britain or of world peace is served by their clearly deliberate intention to provoke war between Britain and the new countries?

The motive of international Socialists is equally clear in their new clamour for war at any price. International Socialism has always taught the people that any form of national action in independence of world conditions was futile, and that the success of Socialism in Britain depended on the universal adoption of their doctrines throughout the world. Now great countries arise which have uprooted in theory and practice the obsolete doctrines of international Socialism, and consequently bar to the British Labour Party all hope of the universal acceptance of their creed, on which they admit alone the success of their cause can depend. So but one hope of the ultimate triumph of their party remains to the leaders of Labour, and that is the overthrow of these new systems by the force of world war. Lightly the Labour leaders appear to be prepared to purchase their political objective in British blood, and to pursue their political vendetta at the price of every interest of Britain and of world peace.

The party which has been built on cant of pacifism today leads the clamour for war, and the party which ever refused Britain arms to defend herself now supports rearmament, not for the defence of Britain, but for the defence by war of international Socialism. Foremost in the van of the new jingoes is the Socialist conscientious objector of 1914. So is presented an edifying spectacle which naturally makes but scant appeal to the ex-serviceman of the last war. He replies with British Union that we have fought Germany once in a British quarrel and we shall not fight her again either in a Socialist or in a Jewish quarrel.

Perversion of the League

In result every high aspiration of the war generation has been frustrated and perverted. The League of Nations, which was the repository of many fine ideals, like the Holy Alliance of the previous century, has been perverted to perform exactly the opposite purpose to that which it was intended to fulfill. The League was meant to overcome the division of Europe, and to eliminate for ever the fatal system of the balance of power, which divided mankind into opposing and contending camps of highly armed and hostile nations. It has been perverted to be a new and more vicious instrument of that system by which Britain, France and Russia, in the name of the League, can mobilise their remaining satellite powers in one balance of a scale, whose other balance, by force of a common original adversity, now holds the armed power of Germany, Italy and Japan.

Despite every aspiration of the war generation and every hope of stricken mankind we are back where we began in a situation which for Britain is more dangerous than before. For the departure by present Government, in their political vendetta, from the sober British policy of pursuing the coincident objectives of peace and British interests has resulted in follies of which British statesman ship has never previously been guilty. Never before in modern times have we placed ourselves in a strategical position so vulnerable that any child could observe it and also apprehend the consequence. We face Germany across the North Sea and Japan in the far seas of our Eastern possessions, while in the Mediterranean route to our Oriental Empire we have succeeded in antagonising at one end the new Spain, and at the other end the Arabs, with an alienated Italy in the middle. With Germany and the Arabs we have quarreled for the sake of the Jews, and with Italy and the new Spain for the sake of international Socialism in an alliance with Russian Communism. Has British statesmanship ever before perpetrated folly on a scale so gigantic, in denial so complete of British interest, security and peace?

Conservative Alliance with Communism

The virtual alliance of Conservative Government in Britain with Communist Government in Russia is at the root of all evil in foreign policy. This curious communion of Conservatism and Communism in the international sphere will not appear so strange to those familiar at home with British Union struggle, who have witnessed again and again the deliberate use by Conservatism of a Communism which, in myopic vision, they do not fear against the creed of the twentieth century, which has excited both the panic and the fury of reaction. Constantly

Conservatism has condoned, excused, and even supported the crimes of Communism when the target was fellow Britons who dared to raise against Conservative betrayal of the people the standard of a new and true patriotism.

Abroad, as at home, Conservatism is willing to use even the vile and bloody instrument of world Communism against the nations of European renaissance. That a virtual alliance exists between the Government of Britain and that of Moscow, with the natural and warm approval of the Socialist opposition, is not today denied. The Franco Soviet Pact has ever been approved by the Conservative Government and the close association of French and British policy, together with the close cooperation of British and Russian policy at Geneva and elsewhere, has almost flaunted in the face of Europe the triple alliance of Britain, France and Russia, to which the overwhelming majority of the British people are completely opposed.

Arms Race Origin

The full historic error of the Franco Soviet Pact can only be appreciated if the chronology of these events is recalled. In November, 1933, the leader of Germany made an offer to Europe which fell into three parts: (1) limitation of German naval strength in fixed ratio to British strength; (2) limitation of German air force to 50 per cent the strength of France; (3) limitation of German army to 300,000 men if France would agree to the same restriction. This offer is on historic record, and also the answer to that offer; for the reply of France, without any protest from Great Britain, was the Franco-Soviet Pact. Only the naval offer was accepted by Britain, with beneficial results, because German naval strength in the outcome of negotiations was limited to a 85 per cent ratio of British strength, and a fatal recurrence of the pre-war naval race between Britain and Germany was averted. The offer of air and land limitation was contemptuously ignored and answered only with the Franco-Soviet Pact, which Germany regarded as an attempt to encircle her. From that moment the sequence of fatality has been clear. Germany armed in a prodigious effort and British rearmament followed.

That Britain should be fully armed in a troubled world, to defend herself from any possible assault, has been a basic principle of British Union long before the National Government, which had criminally neglected our defences, consented to tardy and inefficient rearmament. Disarmament can only be won by world agreement which proportionately reduces the strength of all great nations and leaves the relative strength the same and the immunity from attack the greater. But armament by political parties which have grossly neglected the elementary duty of Government to put Britain in a position of self-defence, as part of an arms race which their blunders have precipitated is a very different matter. Arm we must if other nations are armed, but every effort of statesmanship should seek an end to the menace of arms race, which can only be achieved by world appeasement.

European Division and Eastern Anarchy

In the fatal sequence of events a divided Europe fell an easy and humiliated prey to Oriental anarchy. Germany isolated and encircled, like others in similar predicament, sought support where she could find it, and to the Berlin-Rome axis was added an understanding with Japan. As a result, in face of a divided Europe, Japan was able to cut loose in the Orient, with Great Britain an impotent and humiliated spectator.

A united Europe and a rational policy would at any time have averted the disaster by firm intimation to Japan that north of the Yangtze river, but no further, she was at liberty to do what Britain did in India, and in bringing order where anarchy and bloodshed ruled to find an outlet for her population and access to raw materials. Similarly the dignity and strength of a united Europe could have secured the relatively bloodless suppression of slave trading barbarity in Abyssinia and legitimate expansion for Italy, in full accord with the civilising mission which Britain herself undertook throughout the world. But Europe was divided, and from this division of the mind and spirit a sequence of catastrophe has arisen. Japan, forbidden to expand in Northern China, exploded throughout the Far East, and Italy, forbidden to expand where her legitimate interests were affected in the prevention of slave raiding from adjoining territory, exploded throughout the Near East. The simple lesson of history, and particularly of British history, is that great nations expand or explode. By denying expansion when no British interests were affected we have provoked explosion, and by encouraging to resistance primitive populations whom we had neither the will nor the means to defend, we sacrificed their blood and our own prestige.

We ask what British interest was served by long encouraging resistance to Japan in Northern China, except deference to our Governments Soviet ally, who required that territory as a breeding ground for Oriental Communism, and could exact support in the East against Japan in return for support in the West against Germany. Again we ask what British interest was served by partial and ineffective intervention in the Abyssinian dispute in deference to the clamour of international Socialism at the expense of British dignity and safety. The whole policy throughout has ignored reality. To ignore reality when heading for a precipice is to go over it, and to ignore facts when heading for a war is to incur war.

British Union Principles

So with the lesson in mind of past blunders, which we have consistently opposed, British Union policy in the foreign sphere rests on two principles: (1) to interfere in no quarrels which are not our concern. Britons shall fight for Britain only, and never again shall conscript armies leave these shores in foreign quarrel. Britain we will always defend from any attack, and we will provide the means for that defence, but never again shall British blood be spilt in an alien quarrel; (2) we will give leadership and make contribution to secure the material and spiritual union of Europe, on which alone world peace and British interest in world peace can rest. If, despite that leadership and contribution, the world in madness destroys itself by war we will "Mind Britain's Business" and thereby save our people from that catastrophe.

The New Germany

In that determination it is natural immediately to seek a solution of present difficulties with Germany and the establishment of friendship. That such a solution can be found is plain to anyone who has studied the facts of the new Europe and, therefore, understands the profound difference between the old and the new Germany. The Germany of the Kaiser rested on a system of export capitalism conducted by Judaic finance which challenged us on the markets of the world, and emphasised that challenge with naval rivalry that threatened our Empire. In historic survey the internal forces of that Germany, operating within the international system to which Britain was wedded, made a clash inevitable.

It is, therefore, important to realise that in 15 years of Hitler's struggle a new German psychology was created which rests on a conception exactly the opposite to that of the Kaiser. The new German does not desire a world wide Empire, for he believes that racial deterioration will result from such racial intercourse, and that the new German has another mission in the world than to elevate savages. These are reasons strange for the Englishman to understand, because he knows that the foremost achievements of his race have been evoked in the vast work of Empire building which, in the particular case of his Imperial genius, has led to no such deleterious results. But these facts are important in that they denote no longer a divergence but a community of objective. Britain requires in peace to develop her own Empire, and Germany desires in peace to incorporate within the Reich the Germans of Europe.

The desires of these two powers, therefore, for the first time become not antithetical but complementary. For a strong British Empire throughout the world can be regarded by the new German as a world bulwark against Oriental Communism, and a strong Germany in Europe can be regarded by the new Briton as a European bulwark against the same disruption that invades from the East the life of Western man. From new conceptions in Germany and in Britain can arise a new communion of interest to support the communion that should exist in a common blood.

France and European Solidarity

To this idea the writer, as a friend of the French people, is convinced that France can be attached once she, too, has won freedom from the vendettas of politicians and can be induced to realise that the legitimate expansion of Germany, in directions the opposite to any threat to French interest, is a strength to Europe, and, therefore, a strength to France in securing solidarity against the common menace that comes from the East. If this conception cannot be accepted by financial democratic Government in France it will at least soon arise from the chaos which financial democracy creates in that fair but unhappy country. For it must be admitted that a new sense has come to Germany, and no German in his senses will at infinite sacrifice make a bid to acquire overcrowded territory which belongs to France when his own people and relatively virgin soil summon him in the opposite direction.

Let us put ourselves for a moment in the German position and console ourselves and the French with the reflection that German affairs are no longer conducted by fools but by a man of singular intelligence. By recognition of the fact that the new German interests lie in the East rather than in the West of Europe, British Union does not mean that we seek joint action with Germany in the waging of war against Russia, although we shall forthwith break the present alliance with Russia. On the contrary, we seek peace with all countries, including Russia, and would only join with other powers in action against her if she menaced Great Britain and thus evoked our resolute principle of self-defence. But even the folly of Russian Communism will not challenge the might of an united Europe which, if need arose, would deal with her as easily as with a colonial expedition.

We seek not by war, but by the solidarity of the European spirit and plain commonsense, to secure that legitimate expansion of great nations which can avert the disaster of another and greater explosion. That solution will be found without bloodshed for the good and simple reason that none can resist a combination of the great powers of Europe. Britain, Germany, France and Italy have in this matter a basic community of interest which the victory of the modern movement in Britain can weld into an irrefragable instrument of action in the achievement of peace.

In foreign affairs, as in national life, the leadership principle prevails in reality, and Europe is lost without the united and effective leadership of the Great Powers. Too long we have suffered from the post war delusion that a tiny State, possessing a few thousands of backward population, was not only in theory but in practice the equal of a great nation with millions of advanced peoples to support material power and moral position.

Colonial Question

The great powers must unite and lead to peace, and this final blessing can only come from the victory of British Union in the land that is today the key to world peace. But, in giving leadership, Britain must also make contribution, and long before the colonial question was raised in acute and controversial form British Union declared willingness to hand back to Germany the mandated territories, on simple and clear conditions that they should not be used as naval or air bases against Britain, and that Britain might preserve such facilities as were necessary to her naval and air communications. Such a concession would present no difficulty to a Germany which has already accepted a 35 per cent ratio of our naval strength, and therefore made the maintenance of her potential colonial communications dependent on friendship with Britain. We will not surrender one inch of British territory to any power, but these colonies held in mandate from the League of Nations are not British in law, and in practice we are inhibited from their development for British purposes, with the result that territory, which in restoration would be an outlet and opportunity for Germany, is today a burden and expense to us. Yet the Conservatives, who have betrayed British Empire by throwing open British African possessions as the dumping ground of the world, are ready to jeopardise world peace in clinging to territory we do not require, while neglecting the territory which belongs to us at the expense of infinite sacrifice and heroism of virile generations of the British. So in passing it may be observed that once again the Tory proves himself not only a dog in the manger but also a fool.

Economic Peace

It is clear that the peace of the new world can only rest on material justice and to deny it is to court war. The access of Germany to raw materials and opportunity for outlet and expansion will solve the last material problem of the great powers, for the other dispossessed nations, such as Italy and Japan, have already found a solution by force that the financial democratic world with characteristic folly refused to reason.

Thus in the solution of the German problem it becomes possible for each great nation to build that comparatively self contained civilisation which is the surest guarantee of peace. To those who deny this elementary statement of fact we pose the simple question, what are modern wars about? The answer is clearly that modern wars are economic in the struggle for raw materials and for markets. Consequently if each great nation has access to raw materials, and opportunity to build a market in the purchasing power of their own people, the only effective cause of war in the world is eliminated. The urge to war will go with the suppression of the international struggle for raw materials and markets, and the financial parasite that inflames the fever. Then if the world goes to war the world will indeed be mad, because no reason can exist for war, and Britain with justice will have no part in that madness.

The New Europe

But in truth no such fear need exist, for the reason of the present malady of Europe is not so difficult to diagnose. It is a malady and division of the spirit, which transcends all material differences. Material justice must be done and the new world must be built on the sound reality of a fair economic basis. But deeper than every division of material things is the division of the spirit in the modern Europe. The old world and the new world are divided and they cannot mingle. Either the new world and the old world will collide in disaster or the new world will emerge as the final system of the modern age. Therefore on the fate of Britain depends the fate of mankind.

British Union advances with British policy, method and character suited to this nation and to no other. But we can understand those who in other countries have brought the new world to triumph by policy, method and character suited to their nations as no "democrat" ever can. Because, despite every divergence of policy and difference of national character, we have the same origin in the struggle of our betrayed generation of the war to redeem great nations from corruption, and in common with these others we have passed through the same ordeals and faced the same enemies. This origin of a common experience and determination that great peoples shall not perish from the earth gives us an understanding one of another and a sympathy in the mutual struggle with the dark enemy of mankind that the old world can neither comprehend nor disrupt.

We are British and before all else in our national creed we place Britain and our love of country, but because we love our land we can understand and work with those who love their land. Thus shall be born not only the material union but the spiritual union of the new world.

British Union

SO British Union emerges from the welter of parties and the chaos of the system. To meet an emergency no less menacing than 1914 because it is not so sudden or so universally apparent, British Union summons our people to no less an effort in no less a spirit. Gone in the demand of that hour was the clamour of faction and the strife of section that a great nation might unite to win salvation. A brotherhood of the British was born that in the strength of union was invincible and irresistible.

Today the nation faces a foe more dangerous because he dwells within, and a situation no less grave because to all it is not yet visible. We have been divided and we have been conquered because by division of the British alone we can be conquered. Class against class, faction against faction, party against party, interest against interest, man against man, and brother against brother has been the tactic of the warfare by which the British in the modern age for the first time in their history have been subdued. We have been defeated, too, at a moment in our history when the world was at our feet, because the heritage won for us by the heroism of our fathers affords to the genius of modern science, and the new and unprecedented triumph of the human mind, an opportunity of material achievement leading, through the gift of economic freedom, to a higher spiritual civilisation than mankind in the long story of the human race has yet witnessed. But for the moment the British are defeated and acquiescence in defeat means the end. On the one hand, continued lethargy can lead only to unlimited chaos, ending in ultimate destruction, and, on the other, new effort can open before us a vista of unparalleled and unlimited opportunity.

Humanity can never stand still, and at this moment more than any other in our history the alternatives before a great nation are heroism or oblivion. Can we recapture the union of 1914 and that rapturous dedication of the individual to a cause that transcends self and faction, or are we doomed to go down with the Empires of history in the chaos of usury and sectional greed? That is the question of the hour for which every factor and symptom of the current situation presses decision. Is it now possible by a supreme effort of the British spirit and the human will to arrest what in the light of all past history would appear to be the course of destiny itself? For we have reached the period, by every indication available to the intellect, at which each civilisation and Empire of the past has begun to traverse that downward path to the dust and ashes from which their glory never returned. Every fatal symptom of the past is present in the modern situation, from the uprooting of the people's contact with the soil to the development of usury and the rule of money power, accompanied by social decadence and vice that flaunts in the face or civilisation the doctrine of defeat and decline.

Above the European scene towers in menace Spengler's colossal contribution to modern thought which taught our new generation that a limit is set to the course of civilisations and Empires, and that the course that once is run is for ever closed. Every indication of decadence and decline which he observed as a precursor of the downfall of a civilisation is apparent in the modern scene, and from all history he deduced the sombre conclusion that the effort of "Faustian" man to renew his youth and to recapture the dawn of a civilisation must ever fail. History is on the side of the great philosopher and every sign of the period with fatal recurrence supports his view. His massive pessimism, supported by impressive armoury of fact, rises in challenge and in menace to our generation and our age. We take up that challenge with the radiant optimism born of man's achievements in the new realm of science that the philosopher understood less well than history, and born, above all, of our undying belief in the invincible spirit of that final product of the ages - the modern man.

We salute our great antagonist, from whose great warning we have learnt so much, but we reject utterly the fatality of his conclusion. We believe that modern man with the new genius of modern science within him and the inspiration of the modern spirit to guide him can find the answer to the historic fatality. But to ignore the evidence of the ages and to deride the contribution to human thought of Spengler's great intellect is appropriate only to the pallid "intellectuals" whose emasculated minds lack the energy to study his facts and the courage to face his conclusions. His facts stand, and the only relevant question is whether or not in this epoch of supreme scientific achievement man is armed with the weapons and possesses the will to challenge and to alter the very course of mortal destiny.

It is in immense answer to all past history of human fate that British Union emerges within British Empire and the modern creed in diverse form emerges in all great nations with the decisive challenge of the renaissance of the Western man. Underlying every difference in policy, method, form and character in different nations, the rise of the National Socialist and Fascist doctrine throughout Europe represents in historic determinism the supreme effort of modern man to challenge and overcome the human destiny which in every previous civilisation has ordained irretrievable downfall.

The doctrines of modern disintegration are classic in form and pervade the political parties, which fade from a flaccid and universal "Liberalism" into the sheer disruption and corruption of Socialism serving usury. The doctrinaires of the immediate past come to the aid of political defeatism with the negation of manhood and selfwill and the scientific formulation of surrender as a faith.

In the sphere of economics Marx portrays humanity as the helpless victim of material circumstance, and in the sphere of psychology Freud assists the doctrine of human defeatism with the teaching that selfwill and selfhelp are no longer of any avail, and that man is equally the helpless toy of childish and even pre-natal influence. Marx's "materialist conception of history" tells us that man has ever been moved by no higher instinct than the urge of his stomach, and Freud supports this teaching of man's spiritual futility with the lesson that man can never escape from the squalid misadventures of childhood.

By a fatal conjunction the materialist doctrines of these two Jews have dominated the modern "intellectual" world to the rout and destruction of every value of the spirit. This predestination of materialism has proved in practice even more destructive of the human will and spirit than the old and discredited "predestination of the soul." It has paralysed the intellectual world into the acceptance of surrender to circumstance as an article of faith. To these destructive doctrines of material defeatism our renaissant creed returns a determined answer.

To Marx we say it is true that if we observe the motive of a donkey in jumping a ditch we may discern a desire to consume a particularly luxuriant thistle that grows on the other side. On the other hand, if we observe a man jumping a ditch we may legitimately conclude that he possesses a different and possibly a higher motive.

To Freud we reply that if indeed man has no determination of his own will beyond the idle chances of childhood then every escape from heredity and environment, not only of genius, but of every determined spirit in history, is but a figment of historic imagination.

In answer to the fatalistic defeatism of the "intellectual" world our creed summons not only the whole of history as a witness to the power and motive force of the human spirit, but every evidence and tendency of recent science. Today the whole front of materialism is on the retreat and the scene of modern thought is dominated by the triumph of the spirit. In rout are the little men who taught that nothing could exist that they could not understand. Biology begins again to teach that the wilful determination of the species to rise above the limitations of material environment is the dominating factor in evolution. In psychology the modern school declares that the conscious exertion of man's will prevails over the chance of heredity and environment. In physics the influence of the external to matter, the unknown, in short the spiritual provides phenomena for which the purely material can afford no explanation. In fact, every tendency of modern science assures us that in superb effort the human spirit can soar beyond the restraint of time and circumstance.

So man emerges for the final struggle of the ages the supreme and conscious master of his fate to surmount the destiny that has reduced former civilisations to oblivion even from the annals of time. He advances to the final ordeal armed with weapons of the modern mind that were lacking to the hand of any previous generation in the crisis of a civilisation.

The wonders of our new science afford him not only the means with which to conquer material environment in the ability to wrest wealth in abundance from nature, but, in the final unfolding of the scientific revelation, probably also the means of controlling even the physical rhythm of a civilisation. Man for the first time in human history carries to the crisis of his fate weapons with which he may conquer even destiny. But one compelling necessity remains that he shall win within himself the will to struggle and to conquer. Our creed and our Movement instill in man the heroic attitude to life because he needs heroism.

Our new Britons require the virility of the Elizabethan combined with the intellect and method of the modern technician. The age demands the radiance of the dawn to infuse the wonder of maturity. We need heroism not just for war, which is a mere stupidity, but heroism to sustain us through man's sublime attempt to wrestle with nature and to strive with destiny. To this high purpose we summon from the void of present circumstance the vast spirit of man's heroism. For this shall be the epic generation whose struggle and whose sacrifice shall decide whether man again shall know the dust or whether man at last shall grasp the stars.

We know the answer for we have felt this thing within us. In divine purpose the spirit of man rises above and beyond the welter of chaos and materialism to the conquest of a civilisation that shall be the sum and the glory of the travail of the ages. In that high fate *tomorrow we live*.

Oswald Mosley - May 1938

www.ingramcontent.com/pod-product-compliance
Lightning Source LLC
Chambersburg PA
CBHW070930270326
41927CB00011B/2797